Protecting SQL Server Data

Server Data

By John Magnabosco

First published by Simple Talk Publishing September 2009

Editor: Tony Davis
Copy Editor: Una Campbell
Typeset: Gower Associates.

Table of Contents

ABOUT THE AUTHOR

It all started when my supervisor called me in to her office and handed me an install disk, or more correctly a floppy disk, of a database system and said "*I need you to learn this.*"

This request was not entirely random. I had dabbled with programming off and on throughout my youth with my father's TRS-80 Color Computer. I had worked myself up from delivering coffee and paper clips to the home lending department of a local bank. In that department opportunities arose for me to use my programming skills for automating mundane tasks which was motivated by the desire to never see an IBM Selectric typewriter again.

With this experience behind me, and my supervisor's request pointing the way to my future, I accepted the disk and eagerly began to cross that threshold into the wonderful world of databases. As the years passed and I began to learn and understand normalization, data modelling, data transformation, interface development, data warehousing, backup and recovery, performance and security, my love and passion for this new world quickly grew.

Through this nearly twenty year journey, I have been able to create database systems for the benefit of the banking industry, State government, and more recently heading the Data Services group of one of the fastest growing businesses in the United States.

The technical community was there for me in my formative years offering me deeper explanations of concepts and sharing of ideas with peers. I consider myself very fortunate to give back to this community for the benefit of others who are now where I was many years ago. Through my participation as a co-founder of local organizations such as the **Indianapolis Professional Association for SQL Server** (www.IndyPASS.org) and **IndyTechFest** (www.IndyTechFest.org) my home town of Indianapolis is one of the most active SQL Server communities in the country. In wider circles of influence I have authored articles at DevX.com, provided snack-style instructional videos at JumpstartTV.com and presented on sensitive data solutions at SQL Saturday events.

You can find my latest contribution to the sensitive data dialog at my blog: http://www.simple-talk.com/community/blogs/johnm/default.aspx.

ACKNOWLEDGEMENTS

Books are not written without the help and support of others. I have been very blessed to have a superb network of family, friends and associates who supplied me with the support, encouragement and references, the absence of which would have rendered this project nearly impossible.

Special thanks to: **Tony Davis**, my editor who made the writing process a joy. To my friends and family who supported and encouraged my determination to write this book, specifically: **Brad McGehee**, **Brian Kelley**, **Andy Warren**, **Steve Jones**, **Suzanne Meehle**, **David Leininger**, **Eric Burch**, **Ray Lucas**, **Claire Reagan**, **Casey Reagan**, **Simson Garfinkle**, "*The*" **Jimmy May**, **Tom Pizzato** and, of course, my loving wife **Donna**.

On a lighter note, I would like to offer a special thank you to the **Grateful Dead**, **Jefferson Airplane**, **Bob Dylan** and **Neil Young** for their aid in fueling the creative furnace and defining the soundtrack of this book.

INTRODUCTION

For as long as there has been something to communicate between two persons there has been data. The image of a buffalo hunt inscribed upon the walls of a cave, or a sequence of notches pressed into clay, were early attempts to store this data for later reference. Many generations later, we utilize the data that our ancient ancestors generated to better understand their world and ours.

Today, vast volumes of data are gathered about almost every individual and business. It is the information that we provide when we sign up for an account at our favorite website, send an e-mail, fill out a job application, or apply for a mortgage. It is the information that is stored in a spreadsheet on your employer's server. It is the purchasing habits of customers on Amazon.com or at the neighborhood grocer, stored within their data warehouse.

Some of this data is innocuous, such as the artist's name of an album that is purchased, while some of it is highly sensitive, such as the credit card number that is used in the purchase. This data is stored at various locations, with a range of different levels of security applied to it. When the level of sensitivity is determined to be high, additional steps to secure the data are required to ensure that its disclosure is appropriately handled.

Rules, Regulations and Responsibility

We all, sometimes unwittingly, supply sensitive data about ourselves or the company we work for. When we participate in commerce, file documents with government agencies or share casually in a conversation with a friend, we disclose information about ourselves. It is our responsibility to recognize what is appropriate for the exchange and what is not. While we like to think of our home as our sanctuary, sensitive data is often the target of home robberies. The storage of credit cards, tax returns and other sensitive documents in a secured location is advised.

The consequences of mishandling sensitive data can be severe. Some industries are regulated by privacy acts, defined by a governmental body. The fines placed · on businesses that do not comply with these regulations can be very heavy. Even more damaging is the loss of customer confidence that results when these breaches of security occur. Expensive legal suits are not uncommon for businesses that have suffered a loss of sensitive data.

In all cases, the consequences to the subject of the data are damaging. The laptop that contained a spreadsheet of sensitive information, stolen from an employee's car, can easily result in the company's client becoming a victim of identity theft. The loss of account information from a database can grant to an otherwise unauthorized person access to the client's funds and additional sensitive data. The resolution of the lost sensitive data can cost a lot of money, time and resources which can have a dramatic affect on the client's quality of life and economic stability.

The responsibility of protecting sensitive data is one of no small measure. This responsibility is shared between the providers of sensitive data and the keepers of this valuable asset. The Database Administrator and Security Officer are the last line in defending the data that is entrusted to the business. The Security Officer defines and enforces the policies that provide security from the human element of managing data security. The Data Administrator designs the security architecture and executes the features of the database that keep the data in the hands of the good-guys.

Overcoming Encryptionphobia

The general topic of protecting data and the database is quite an expansive one. A few of the tactics used in this effort include server hardening, user access maintenance, managing data in memory, socket management, prevention of SQL injection, development of polices that protect employees from social engineering attempts as well as practices that protect a business from their own personnel. While critical to the overall security effort these items are not within the scope of this specific book.

The focus of this book is protecting sensitive data that is "at rest" and stored within our SQL Server database. Devices and methods that protect data externally from the database, such as firewalls, secured network connections and user interface cryptography methods, are all important, but the overall success of your efforts to protect sensitive data will depend upon how well you guard the data in your databases. In order to do this, the DBA needs to employ the encryption and obfuscation techniques that are available within SQL Server, and that are discussed throughout this book.

I recently had a conversation regarding data security and encryption, to which the closing statement was "encryption is just another way for data to be lost". It is a worryingly common sentiment. In any given conversation about encryption it is nearly certain that the question "What happens if the key is lost?" will be asked. Of course, it is a valid concern. After all, a lost key means that the encrypted data cannot be decrypted and therefore is lost. However, the fear of the "lost key" is not a valid reason to avoid encryption altogether.

When I was a student, a recurring nightmare of mine was the forgotten locker combination. The scenario would be that I was rushing through the halls on my way to a very important examination; but, first there was "something" I needed out of my locker. As I began to spin the dial on the lock of my locker I soon realized that its combination had slipped my memory. In desperation I began trying random numbers in the hope that I would guess the code. A stream of students making their way into their classrooms buffeted me to a fro elevating my anxiety. The hallway gradually cleared and the din of chatting reduced to the clapping echo of the final student's footsteps. Thankfully, this never happened in real life.

This is the fear of not being able to access something of value when it is needed. It is the fear of the fragile nature of our memories, and of the inability to recall the "special code" in a time of need. It explains why passwords are found scribbled on a Post-it® note and stuck to the monitor screen. It is a key reason that more advanced protection methods for sensitive data, such as encryption, are avoided.

If encryption is implemented without careful planning and without a maintenance strategy, it can become a hairy mess; but isn't this also true of any aspect of data and database administration? Without regular backups and careful attention to data integrity, a database is at a high risk of data loss, regardless of whether or not you use encryption.

Encryption requires careful consideration of what should be protected and the extent of its application. Granting permissions to the keys, and performing any necessary schema modifications to accommodate the encrypted values, are also a part of the implementation process Once encryption is implemented it requires periodic maintenance of retiring aging encryption keys with fresh ones. This practice ensures the continued effectiveness of the keys.

A fundamental aspect of the whole process is backing up the encryption keys and storing them in a safe location. If these practices are followed, the DBA's answer to the question "What happens if the key is lost?" should be exactly the same as the answer they'd give if asked the question "What happens if data is corrupted or lost due to a disk failure": I will restore it from backup. Failure to do so in either case may result in a new DBA job posting.

I'm hoping, with this book to address some of the concerns and confusion surrounding encryption, and other data protection methods. I hope to hear the question "What happens if I do not encrypt my sensitive data?" occur more often in my conversations regarding data security. I hope to see the fear of the "lost key" displaced by fear of data loss due to unauthorized disclosure, which will not only result in the leakage of sensitive data but also exposure to the data being fraudulently modified. Encryption is one of the most valuable weapons with which that battle can be won.

What this Book covers

The topics covered in this book will introduce the basic concepts of sensitive data and offer some solutions that focus on the data itself. This includes:

- **Defining sensitive data**: Clearly understanding the characteristics that define sensitive data is the first step in the journey toward protecting it. This topic will cover the legal definitions of sensitive data and provide several real-world examples of data that fit this category.

- **Data classification**: Born from the understanding of sensitive data is the process of identifying the columns within the tables of our database that contain it. It is through this process that data is classified so that the appropriate security methods can be applied.

- **Database schema considerations**: The design of a database's tables, columns and their relationship to each other is a key step in the process of developing a database. There are many things to consider when approaching this design; one of which is effectiveness and efficiency of storing sensitive data.

- **Encryption**: Once sensitive data is identified and appropriately stored it is ready to be protected. Cryptography is one method in which the plain text that is submitted to the database is transformed into a series of values that is unrecognizable to readers who do not have the key to decrypt it.

- **Other obfuscation methods**: Encryption is not the only way to hide data from prying eyes. There are other methods that can be used when the use of cryptography is too strong or inefficient. This topic will explore these options as well as ways to identify when someone is snooping around in search of unprotected data.

While the topics such as defining sensitive data and data classification can be applied to any database platform, all database specific features presented are within the context of Microsoft SQL Server 2005 and Microsoft SQL Server 2008.

The release of SQL Server 2005 introduced features, such as cell-level encryption, that were focused on protecting sensitive data. SQL Server 2008 continued that trend with features such as Transparent Data Encryption, the ability to audit more fully data manipulation language (DML) and other activities within the database.

It is my hope that you find this book very useful in your efforts to protect the valuable assets that are contained within your database.

Code Download

Throughout this book are code samples that use a sample HomeLending database for illustrative purposes. The specific details regarding the design of the sample database can be found in the "Introducing the HomeLending Database" section of Chapter 2.

To download the entire HomeLending database and all code samples presented in this book, visit the following URL:

http://www.simple-talk.com/RedGateBooks/JohnMagnabosco/HLSchema.zip

Details regarding the download, creation and execution of the code samples can be found in Appendix B of this book, as well as being documented with the downloaded code samples.

Feedback

I have always found a book to be more valuable when discussion surrounds its reading. It is even more beneficial when the author is available for correspondence. If you have any questions or feedback in regard to this book or the scripts that were provided, please contact me at encryptionphobia@live.com.

Chapter 1: Understanding Sensitive Data

Data is a form of currency. As members of society, we provide information about ourselves to gain access to services and goods that we desire. We collect information about others in order to market our services and obtain verification of identity. As Database Professionals it is our lifeblood. We labor daily to store, backup, transfer, transform, share, report, analyze and protect data. Ultimately, our primary concern is protection of the data's integrity, availability and confidentiality.

In order to effectively protect our sensitive data, it is critical that we understand the characteristics that define that data as being sensitive. In this chapter, we will explore the characteristics that make data sensitive, present specific examples of sensitive data and discuss some of the weapons available to the Database Administrators that are employed to protect it.

What Makes Data Sensitive?

Subjectively, sensitive data can be defined simply as information that the holder does not wish to share publicly. A wild array of information could fall into this category, depending upon the motivation of the holder at any given time. This could include the refusal to supply their phone number, birth date, or their adoration of a not-so-popular celebrity.

Objectively, there are laws, regulations and industry standards that provide a solid framework for defining sensitive data. A few examples of these are the United Kingdom's Data Protection Act of 1998, Canada's Personal Information Protection and Electronic Information Act and the United States Department of Health and Human Services' Privacy Rule of the Health Insurance Portability and Accountability Act.

Personal, Identifiable and Sensitive Data

The terminology used when referring to the protection of information can be confusing. Gaining an understanding of the subtleties of these terms will provide the clarity needed to identify the sensitivity of our data.

The three most common terms used to describe this information are:

- Personal data
- Identifiable data
- Sensitive data.

Personal Data

The term "personal data" is very broad in scope. It can apply to any data that pertains to an individual, and does not necessarily reflect its level of sensitivity. Examples of personal data are an individual's hair color, musical preferences, criminal history, cell phone number, and the high school they attended.

According to the United Kingdom's Data Protection Act of 1998, personal data is defined as:

> *"... data which relates to a living individual who can be identified – a) from those data, or b) from those data and other information which is in the possession of, or is likely to come in the possession of, the data controller."*

Depending upon the definitions that are used in the regulations, standards and policies that are being considered, data that may otherwise be considered a low sensitivity risk could be escalated.

Identifiable Data

Identifiable data is a more specific term than personal data. It applies specifically to information that uniquely defines an individual. For example, my personal data may indicate that I am a fan of the Beatles; but there are millions of other people who share that interest. My federal identification number, however, is assigned only to me and through this unique number my identity can be verified.

20

In a memorandum to the Executive Departments and Agencies of the United States Federal Government, from the White House, the definition of identifiable data is:

> *"... Information which can be used to distinguish or trace an individual's identity, such as their name, social security number, biometric records, etc. Alone, or when combined with other personal or identifying information which is linked or linkable to a specific individual such as date and place of birth, mother's maiden name, etc."*

Data that is defined as identifiable requires an elevated effort in regard to its protection, and the prevention of improper disclosure.

Sensitive Data

Sensitive data is a term that includes identifiable data, but also extends to information that may be considered private, or to have societal and economic consequences if improperly disclosed. It is also information that could cause harm to an organization if it is improperly disclosed. This type of data includes political opinions, religious beliefs, mental or physical condition, criminal record, financial status, intellectual property, organizational membership, codes and passwords that grant access to accounts, and information of national security.

According to the United Kingdom's Data Protection Act of 1998, Sensitive data is defined as:

> *"... personal data consisting of information as to – a) the racial or ethnic origin of the data subject, b) his political opinions, c) his religious beliefs or other beliefs of a similar nature, d) whether he is a member of a trade union ..., e) his physical or mental health or condition, f) his sexual life, g) the commission or alleged commission by him of any offence, or h) any proceedings for any offence committed or alleged to have been committed by him, the disposal of such proceedings or the sentence of any court in such proceeding."*

In the definition provided by the Data Protection Act, it is specific to information of an individual; but sensitive data spans beyond the scope of the individual and includes businesses, organizations and nations. Data that is considered sensitive will always require additional efforts to protect it and prevent unauthorized disclosure.

Implications of Data Theft

Other motivating factors in determining data sensitivity include the propensity of being subject to identity theft, plus consideration of individual privacy, and of national security.

Identity Theft

Identity theft is the process of obtaining a person's identity for the purpose of committing fraudulent activities. In 1998, the United States Congress passed the Identity Theft and Assumption Deterrence Act, which made identity theft a federal felony. The United States Federal Trade Commission reported that, in the year 2007, over 1.2 billion dollars were lost as the result of identity theft and related fraudulent activities.

The crime of stealing a person's identity can begin with the disclosure of data as seemingly as innocent as a person's name and birth date. This information may be all that is needed to identify one John Smith from the million other John Smiths. With that information in hand, other identifying data could be obtained through research, hacking and social engineering efforts. Ultimately, the "hacker" may use this information to obtain fraudulent forms of identity verification, such as a passport, credit card, or driver's license.

Terrorists, illegal immigrants, and criminals often deflect suspicion by assuming the identity of unsuspecting law abiding citizens. It is through the protection of sensitive data that the efforts of the identity thief are confounded. The livelihood of the person that is the subject of the sensitive data is often dependent upon the methods employed to secure sensitive data in the database.

Privacy

One of the cornerstones of a free society is the freedom of an individual to reveal or withhold personal information in a selective manner. It is through this selective disclosure that we protect ourselves from false accusations from other persons or governmental entities. This Privacy also allows freedom of speech and individual thought to prevail.

Without this protection, any action that a person takes, and every statement that a person makes, can easily be taken out of context and used to damage their reputation, or potentially threaten their freedom.

In October 1998 the European Commission issued the Directive on Data Protection that restricted the sharing of personal data with countries that do not comply with their standard for privacy protection. Later, the United States Department of Commerce and the European Commission formed the Safe Harbor Network to aid organizations in attaining compliance of privacy policies.

Data that is considered private is not limited to identifiable data but also electronic communications, documents, memos, medical histories, performance reviews, purchasing history and other similar data that is stored in a database. The protection, access and retention of this sensitive data are critical elements of the Database Administrator's responsibilities.

National Security

Some of the most sensitive information concerns national security. Disclosure of such information to the wrong people can threaten a country's stability, or possibly even its continued existence. Military information is typically the first type of data that is protected on grounds of national security. Other data in this realm may include trade agreement details, scientific discoveries that have global consequences if disclosed improperly, and the schedules of key figures of the government.

During World War II, the popular slogan of "Loose lips sink ships" reminded citizens that sharing even seemingly harmless information could have dire consequences to the troops that were fighting in the war. The information provided in the letters sent to the troops from home could have fallen into enemy hands and been used against the allied forces' efforts on the frontline. What was true of wartime letters is also true for sensitive data that is stored in databases.

If you are a DBA within the military or government, or a civilian business that handles data from the military or government, you need to have a clear understanding of the data handling policies that have been established by the military or government agency in order to protect this special form of sensitive data.

Compliance with Regulations

Federal, State and local governments establish laws and guidelines that pertain to sensitive data. Some of these laws are industry specific, such as the United State's Financial Privacy Act of 1978, which pertains to data that is specific to financial records and account information of a financial institution's customers. Others are broader in their scope, such as the United Kingdom's Data Protection Act of 1998, which pertains to any entity that obtains, stores and discloses sensitive data.

Compliance of laws and regulations are monitored through regulatory agencies and audits. The consequences of non-compliance range from denial of a benefit, to the levying of significant fines and, in some situations, prison terms.

In addition to governmental regulations are standards that are defined by industries. These industries enforce compliance with these standards in the provisions and to utilization of their services. Many of these laws, regulations and standards define how sensitive data is to be stored and disclosed.

An example of such a standard is the one developed by the major credit card companies, called the Payment Card Industry Data Security Standard (PCI DSS). Requirement 3 of the PCI DSS designates the card holder's name, the primary account number, expiration date, service code and the authentication data as being sensitive data and defines how this information is to be stored and protected. The PCI DSS specifically states that encryption, hashing or truncation is to be utilized for storage of the primary account number. Violation of the standard results in significant fines and the restriction of credit card processing.

As a DBA, an understanding of these requirements is critical to the compliance efforts of your organization. In many cases it is only the DBA who has the level of knowledge that is required to recognize what is involved in meeting these specifications.

Types of Sensitive Data

The following sections provide some specific examples of data that is generally considered sensitive by laws, regulations or industry standards.

24

Government Assigned Identification

Throughout the world, individuals and businesses are provided with various identification numbers, by their respective governments. This data is important to governments for validation of citizenship, work status, taxation, claiming of benefits, general identification and licensing. The following are a few examples of identification numbers that are assigned by governments around the world:

- Driver's License Number
- Passport Data
- Social Security Number (USA)
- Employer Identification Number (USA)
- Individual Taxpayer Identification Number (USA)
- Preparer Taxpayer Identification Number (USA)
- Permanent Resident Alien Number (USA)
- Value Added Tax Identification Number (EU)
- Unique Tax Payer Reference (UK)
- National Insurance Number (UK)
- Company Tax Reference (UK)
- General Index Reference Number (India)
- Permanent Account Number (India)
- Tax File Number (Australia).

All of these pieces of data are to be considered sensitive. When a given identification number is used widely, beyond its original intended purpose, the potential damage from unauthorized disclosure increases.

For example, consider the Social Security Number, first introduced in the United States by President Franklin Roosevelt in 1935. Its initial intent was to identify a tax payer who was paying the Social Security Tax. Attached to this tax are various benefits such as retirement and disability benefits. However, over the decades this number became much more widely used as a way for organizations, businesses, hospitals and educational institutions to uniquely identify a US Citizen.

Due to this extended usage, the unauthorized disclosure of the Social Security Number opens up a Pandora's Box of possibilities for fraudsters. The Social Security Number is associated with credit reports, financial records, medical history, criminal history, tax records, passports, birth certificates, public records, voter registration, professional licenses and many other items that are used to validate identity.

Laws have been enacted over the years at the Federal level, such as the United States' Gramm-Leach-Bliley Act, and at the state level, such as Indiana Code § 9-24-6-2, in an effort to curtail use of the Social Security Number beyond its intended purpose. However, there remain many legacy systems that utilize the Social Security Number to uniquely identify a customer's record.

As a DBA, keep an eye out for the use of any government assigned identification as the primary key, or as a unique identifier, for an individual or business. Strongly discourage the use of sensitive data for this purpose. It is far preferable to use a system-generated value that does not have meaning beyond the database, such as using an auto-numbering column or a GUID (globally unique identifier), to define the primary key for a customer.

Biometric Data

Upon and within ourselves we contain data that can be used as a form of identity verification. This information is called **biometric data**. Persons who have been severely burned are often identified through the use of dental records. When data such as the number of teeth, their placement within the mouth, the various types of dental work that have been performed on them, is properly documented, it can be used to positively determine our identity.

There are many ways to categorize the different types of biometric data but, in a nutshell, it can be lumped into two primary types: **physiological** and **behavioral**.

Physiological biometrics is the information that pertains directly to our bodies. These are the measurements of the tiny, and not-so tiny, features that make us unique in this world of over six billion people. Below are a few specific examples:

- Fingerprints
- Finger or hand geometry

- Facial geometry
- Iris or retina patterns
- Ear geometry
- Dental geometry
- DNA.

Behavioral biometrics is the information that pertains to the uniqueness of our physical motions. This type of biometric data is used in voice recognition software. Banks have been using signature cards for many years to verify whether a check or withdrawal slip is fraudulent. Below are a few specific examples of behavioral biometrics:

- Signature
- Typing patterns
- Voice patterns
- Stride, or walking patterns.

Biometric data is permanent and, correctly or otherwise, is regarded as nearly irrefutable evidence of a person's identity. As such, this type of data should be considered sensitive.

The Biometric Institute in Australia has established an industry standard called the "Biometric Institute Privacy Code" in response to the Australian Privacy Act of 1988. This code presents guidelines for access control, protection in storage and disposal of biometric data. As a DBA, these aspects of biometric data demand careful attention.

Medical Data and History

Each visit to the doctor, dentist, hospital or specialist generates data about our physical and mental condition. Also, when an invoice is generated for the services rendered, and we make payment, there are records created that present a historical record of our payment activity. This data is considered sensitive.

Disclosing this information to the general public presents opportunities for denial of insurance coverage, denial of employment, denial of residence, denial of access to public facilities and, in some cases, social scrutiny and ridicule.

According to the United States Department of Health and Human Services' Privacy Rule of the Health Insurance Portability and Accountability Act (HIPAA) the data that is considered protected within this rule are:

- Information that identifies an individual
- An individual's medical condition
- An individual's health care history
- An individual's history of payment for health care.

In the United Kingdom Act of Parliament titled the Data Protection Act of 1998 the protection of sensitive personal data includes the condition of an individual's mental or physical health.

Access control is a critical aspect of maintaining this type of data in a database. Many times this data is requested by researchers. For their purposes access to aggregated data is sufficient. This aggregated data should not include identifiable or other sensitive data.

Student Education Data

Students have a unique set of data that is considered sensitive, beyond the standard identifiable data, such as federal tax identification number, name, address and birth date.

In the United States, any educational agency or institution that receives Federal Funding by the United States Department of Education is subject to the Federal Educational Rights and Privacy Act (FERPA). This law is designed to protect the privacy of students.

In this act, a school must seek permission from the student to disclose their academic data to another party. This data includes:

- Student's grade history
- Focus of study
- Attendance of official school events
- Personal information such as government assigned identification and address information
- Disability records.

In addition to FERPA, there is the Children's Online Privacy Protection Act of 1998 which is designed to prevent identifiable information about children, under the age of thirteen, from being published on a website or an online service, such as e-mail, message board or chat room. This information includes:

- First and last name
- Home address
- Email address
- Telephone number
- Social Security Number
- Identifiers used in data collection efforts.

While the Children's Online Privacy Protection Act is not specific to educational records, many student activities include children under the age of thirteen; therefore this regulation often coincides with FERPA.

As in many cases when dealing with data that is regulated, strict control of access to data is vital in its protection. Careful consideration as to how this data is disclosed, whether it be on a report or presented on a screen, is an important role of the DBA.

Employment Records

The Human Resources department of any given business contains a myriad of sensitive information on each of their employees. In this environment, there are many internal policies and regulations to which one must adhere to protect this data from those who seek its disclosure.

The United States Department of Health and Human Services' Privacy Rule of the Health Insurance Portability and Accountability Act (HIPAA) is an example of one of the regulations that also applies to employee data. In addition to HIPAA, there are many other privacy regulations that affect, and define, the sensitivity of employment data. Some are at the federal level, such as the United State's Federal Privacy Act of 1974, and some at the state level, such as the California Information Practices Act, as well as various internal corporate policies that are specific to a given business.

The following are a few examples of data that is considered sensitive when considering information regarding employees and their jobs:

- Salary details and history
- Insurance benefits and beneficiary information
- Direct deposit account information
- Job description details
- Background check results
- Reference validation
- Exit interviews.

This data should not only be controlled in its disclosure to persons both outside and inside the company. IT Professionals that are supporting the systems of the Human Resources Department should not have access to plain text information regarding their fellow employees. The temptation to run a query to compare their salaries to their co-workers is great and is an abuse of their role.

As the gatekeeper of this information, the DBA should consider obfuscation methods, discussed later in this book, to make this data unavailable to those who need to maintain the systems that contain this data.

Communication Data

The fourth amendment to the United States Constitution states:

> *"The right of the people to be secure in their persons, houses, papers, and effects, against unreasonable searches and seizures, shall not be violated, and no Warrants shall issue, but upon probable cause, supported by Oath or affirmation, and particularly describing the place to be searched, and the persons or things to be seized."*

It is in support of this amendment that the Stored Communications Act (SCA) was developed, which protects stored electronic communication data from unauthorized access and destruction by the government, businesses or other entities.

In 2002, The Council of the European Union passed directive 2002/58/EC which specifically states in regard to the storage of electronic communications:

"... Measures should be taken to prevent unauthorised access to communications in order to protect the confidentiality of communications, including both the contents and any data related to such communications, by means of public communications networks and publicly available electronic communications services ... The prohibition of storage of communications and the related traffic data by persons other than the users or without their consent is not intended to prohibit any automatic, intermediate and transient storage of this information in so far as this takes place for the sole purpose of carrying out the transmission in the electronic communications network and provided that the information is not stored for any period longer than is necessary for the transmission and for traffic management purposes, and that during the period of storage the confidentiality remains guaranteed ..."

Data that is stored in a database, file system, or within an application that consists of communications between parties, should be protected carefully. Within these communications could reside other personal, identifiable and sensitive data, or dialog that could be misconstrued or used against the parties involved in the court of law.

In some cases, as in the directive 2002/58/EC, there are some communications that are restricted from being stored beyond their transmission. Other federal and state regulations, such as The United States' Sarbanes-Oxley Act of 2002 (SOX), define data retention periods that must be followed; therefore, the consideration of whether to capture or to permit the deletion and modification of communication data is important for the DBA.

Financial Data

In the United States, the Right to Financial Privacy Act of 1978 prevents financial institutions from disclosing financial records to government authorities without a warrant, subpoena or customer authorization. In this law the definition of a financial record is:

"... original of, a copy of, or information known to have been derived from, any record held by a financial institution pertaining to a customer's relationship with the financial institution."

This regulation requires strict access controls on financial data, and on the customer's personal and identifiable data. There are also aspects of this regulation that define how disclosure of this information can be gained through warrants, judgments and court orders.

The Gramm-Leach-Bliley Act (GLBA), which was enacted by the United States Congress in 1999, defines various steps that are required by financial institutions to ensure the security of their customers' non-public data. These steps include limitations of the use of this data, and establishing policies that provide protection from social engineering efforts. The GLBA's definition of non-public is:

> *"... personally identifiable financial information – (i) provided by a consumer to a financial institution; (ii) resulting from any transaction with the consumer or any service performed for the consumer; or (iii) otherwise obtained by the financial institution ..."*

Among the requirements of this regulation is the ability for a customer to opt out of the sharing of information with third parties that are unaffiliated with the financial institution. Also, the development of processes to monitor and test security measures implemented.

The Payment Card Industry Data Security Standard (PCI DSS) is not a regulation of law, but a set of standards that have been defined by representatives from American Express, Discover Financial Services, Master Card, Visa and JCB International. The businesses and organizations that accept and transmit credit card transactions are subject to these standards.

Within these standards the following data is considered sensitive:

- Card holder's name
- Expiration date
- Service code
- Primary account number (PAN)
- Validation codes
- Personal identification number (PIN).

According to the PCI Data Security Standards (PCI DSS) a portion of this sensitive data, specifically the PAN, is explicitly required to be encrypted, hashed or truncated if stored. Other data such as the PIN, and the entirety of the contents of the magnetic strip upon the credit card, are not permitted to be stored beyond the duration of the transaction.

Trade Secrets

Trade secrets are an important aspect of corporate competition. It may be the quality, or design, of a product that gives it an edge over similar products in the market. The formula for the syrup used in Coca-Cola is a trade secret. Due to this unique formula it has a distinct flavor which is different than Pepsi Cola or RC Cola. Depending upon your taste preferences, it is this trade secret that may draw you to purchase Coca-Cola over the other brands, and develops consumer loyalty.

In the United States, there is a law called the "Uniform Trade Secrets Act" (UTSA), designed to provide some uniformity to the definition of a trade secret, as well as provide some guidelines around what constitutes the misappropriation of trade secrets. This law defines a trade secret as:

> *"... information, including a formula, pattern, compilation, program device, method, technique, or process, that: (i) derives independent economic value, actual or potential, from not being generally known to, and not being readily ascertainable by proper means by, other persons who can obtain economic value from its disclosure or use, and (ii) is the subject of efforts that are reasonable under the circumstances to maintain its secrecy."*

In addition to the UTSA law there is the Economic Espionage Act of 1996 that makes the disclosure of trade secrets to unauthorized parties a federal crime:

> *"... Whoever, with intent to convert a trade secret, that is related to or included in a product that is produced for or placed in interstate or foreign commerce, to the economic benefit of anyone other than the owner thereof, and intending or knowing that the offense will, injure any owner of that trade secret, knowingly -- (1) steals, or without authorization appropriates, takes, carries away, or conceals, or by fraud, artifice, or deception obtains such information; (2) without authorization copies, duplicates, sketches, draws, photographs, downloads, uploads, alters, destroys, photocopies, replicates, transmits, delivers, sends, mails, communicates, or conveys such information; (3) receives, buys, or possesses such information, knowing the same to have been stolen or appropriated, obtained, or converted without authorization; ..."*

Laws regarding trade secrets are often focused on the disclosure of information rather than the storage of it; but the control of disclosure begins with protecting the stored data. As with any sensitive data the access controls to the data are highly critical in any protection efforts. Granting access to only those users who need access to the sensitive data, on an as needed basis, is a good practice. Careful consideration of how data is presented when including trade secret information on reports or spreadsheets that are drawn from databases is also an important aspect.

Group Dynamics of Sensitive Data

A standard wooden spoon that sits within the kitchen drawer is rather harmless and holds no special intrigue. A two liter bottle of cola offers little more excitement beyond its momentary burst of enthusiasm when first opened; but when the harmless wooden spoon is dipped into the boring two liter bottle of cola it is bedlam! A tall column of caramel liquid rushes towards the sky and drapes its stickiness over everything within its range.

A similar effect can be achieved with data. As a single piece of data, your date of birth is just one of the 365 days that are on everyone's calendar. However, given added context, such as your name, the date of birth becomes data that is highly valuable to someone who is attempting to steal your identity. From this small start, an identity thief can discover additional information that can be used to make their exposure of your sensitive data complete. Add your mother's maiden name, along with place of birth, and a certified copy of a birth certificate could be obtained which can result in the acquiring of valid passports, driver's licenses and Social Security cards.

The PCI DSS recognizes this dynamic when it states that the cardholder's name, service code and expiration date are required to be protected when it is stored in conjunction with the primary account number (PAN). Otherwise employing protection methods for the cardholder's name, service code and expiration date are optional for compliance with PCI DSS.

When reviewing a database for the consideration of applying protection methods, and implementing access controls, keep this dynamic in mind. Additional protection, abstraction and obfuscation methods may be required even if the columns involved have been assigned a low or medium sensitivity class. Some solutions for reducing the sensitive group dynamic might include:

- **Careful consideration of the data that is being captured** in the database. For example, it is not uncommon to capture the full name of an individual in a database. However, there may be times when the last name, or initials, are all that are required for the purpose of the system.

- **Capturing only a portion of personal data.** For example, storing only the birth year portion of a birth date. Another option might be to capture the birth date in an obscure format such as Julian date. For example, the date of 06/03/2009 00:00:00.000 is the Julian date of 2454985.50000.

- **Applying a one-way hash to personal information** such as mother's maiden name. By doing so the value will never be readable in plain text and yet the ability to compare an entered value remains. This will be covered in more detail in Chapter 7 of this book.

Data at Rest and Data in Transit

Data at rest refers to data that is stored, archived or residing on backup media. Data in transit refers to data that is traversing a network, or residing in memory. Both states of data have their security concerns and methods of threat mitigation.

The PCI DSS is a good example of an industry standard that presents the requirements of securing sensitive data differently for data at rest and data in transit. Requirement 3 of the PCI DSS focuses on data storage, access control, and readability of sensitive data while in storage, as well as encryption key management. These techniques are focused on data at rest. Requirement 4 of the PCI DSS focuses on the use of security protocols, wireless networks and encryption, which are focused on data in transit.

When considering protection methods, keep in mind that many methods that are designed to protect data at rest are not necessarily sufficient for data in transit. For example, SQL Server 2008 offers a feature called Transparent Data Encryption (TDE). This feature encrypts the physical files of a database, its transaction logs and back up files. When data that is encrypted with TDE is queried it is decrypted and stored in the memory cache as plain text. There are critics of this feature who may view this as a flaw in its design; but when you consider that the scope of this feature was to fulfill the requirements of protecting data at rest, and not data in transit, you realize that this feature is extremely effective, and is not intended to be the silver bullet for all data security concerns. More details in regard to the Transparent Data Encryption feature of SQL Server 2008 will be covered in Chapter 6 of this book.

The methods of protecting sensitive data that are presented in this book are primarily focused on the protection of data at rest. In doing so, it is not to suggest that the protection of sensitive data in transit is less of a concern when managing your data security strategies. The DBA should be aware of the threats to sensitive data in both states, when preparing solutions for those who consume the data they manage. Typically the strategies of protecting data in transit fall upon the shoulders of the Network Administrator who manages the physical servers and network connections. The protection of data at rest is often in the realm of the DBA who architects database schemas, performs backups and manages access to the databases. Therefore, it is valuable to present solutions to the challenges that are unique to the DBA.

Shields and Swords

It is not an exaggeration to say that we, as DBAs, are at war with data thieves. In our possession are assets that are valuable. The hackers, phishers, rumor mongers and identity thieves all want to possess these assets. They employ every weapon and strategy that is available to them, including social engineering, brute force attacks on databases, dumpster diving, burglary, interception of mail, network sniffing, and so on, to succeed in their efforts.

Defending data is a "war", and a war cannot be won by employing only a single weapon. As DBAs, we have many weapons and strategies available to us to protect our sensitive data, each of which will be covered in more detail throughout this book.

Data Classification

The beginning of data protection is the knowledge of the data that we keep. If we are unaware that we hold sensitive data in our database we will not make the effort to secure it. The process of data classification is our path to enlightenment.

Through data classification we categorize each column within our database according to its level of sensitivity. Based upon these categories, protection methods can be consistently applied and managed.

Schema Architecture

Strategic storage of data and the abstraction of the underlying organization of the database provide a way to reduce the risk of full disclosure of sensitive data. Increasing the amount of knowledge and persistence required to disclose sensitive data outside of the established methods reduces the players involved on the battlefield.

Normalization offers an efficient way of storing data within a relational database. For the benefit of securing sensitive data normalization offers the separation of sensitive data from data that is considered less sensitive. This separation increases the level of disclosure that has to occur to make the sensitive data useful to the data thief.

SQL Server offers a linked servers feature which presents the opportunity to expand the benefits of normalization across multiple physical servers; thus increasing the requirements to gain access to the sensitive data that is stored in the separate database server.

Views and database object schemas are features of the database that offer layers of abstraction of the underlying schema of the database which provide a way to protect sensitive data and more effectively manage access to it.

Obfuscation

Rendering data unreadable or incomplete for the benefit of hiding its true contents is known as obfuscation. Cryptography is also a common term used to reference this practice.

Encryption is a popular method of obfuscation. Through this method an algorithm is used to render the data unreadable. To return the data to its readable format requires a key that is available to a select few individuals.

Hashing, which is also known as one-way encryption, is another weapon available to the Database Administrator. Like encryption, this process uses an algorithm to render the data unreadable; but once the data is encrypted it cannot be returned to its readable format. The disclosure of the readable value is obtained by comparing hashed values of the data and entered value.

Truncation, masking and encoding are also methods of obfuscation that reduce the readability of the sensitive data therefore reducing its risk and value when disclosed. These methods of obfuscation are often the last line in the defense of sensitive data. If there is a breach in security that allows an unauthorized individual to gain access to the data, these methods will render that data unusable.

Monitoring

The battle of securing sensitive data is a continuous one. The adversaries of our security efforts are persistent. Without the effort of maintaining or improving our protection methods they will become circumvented and our sensitive data will be exposed. The process of monitoring the activities that occur in our databases is a way to measure the effectiveness of our protection methods and identify when it is time to improve them.

SQL Server 2008 offers a new auditing feature that provides a means of monitoring a wide variety of actions that occur within the database. The notification of specific events though the Database Mail feature provides a way for the Database Administrator to react to occurrences as they happen.

Honeycombing a database offers a tactic of placing decoy tables within the database schema that give the appearance of unprotected sensitive data. By applying an audit on these decoy tables the Database Administrator can be immediately notified of a user that is snooping around for sensitive data.

Summary

An understanding of the data that has been entrusted to your business, and the methods available to protect it, is fundamental to the effectiveness of your security strategy. With this understanding we can turn our attention to the classification of the data and the mechanism in which this data is stored: the database.

CHAPTER 2: DATA CLASSIFICATION AND ROLES

The systematic arrangement of items, based upon their similarity, is a natural tendency of humans. We categorize living beings into classes, establish genres of entertainment, define nationalities of people, specify types of food and designate criteria of celestial objects. This practice is referred to as **classification**.

The process of classification of sensitive data is that of identifying patterns and similarities between different types of data so that we can define a common approach to securing it. Having classified our data, we will be able to apply the appropriate level of security to it, and communicate the policies that determine how the data will be handled by its users.

In this chapter, using an example HomeLending database, we will:

- Define some simple "sensitivity classes" that can be used to group columns of data according to their level of sensitivity.

- Create Database Roles through which we can control access to each class of data.

- Assign membership of each role.

- Use SQL Server extended properties to assign a sensitivity class to each database column.

Finally, we'll discuss how this simple classification might be extended for more specific requirements, and how we define and allocate the data handling policies appropriate for each class of data.

Introducing the HomeLending Database

Before we begin in earnest, it will be useful to review a few details regarding our sample HomeLending database which will be used to illustrate the topics in this book. This will be a simplified version of a database that might be used by a financial institution for the purpose of managing the home equity and mortgage loan application process. A copy of the script that will create this database in your own instance of SQL Server can be obtained from the following URL:

http://www.simple-talk.com/RedGateBooks/JohnMagnabosco/HLSchema.zip

The following illustration shows the database schema for the HomeLending database. This schema is based upon the Uniform Residential Loan Application, or commonly referenced as the Fannie Mae 1003 form, which is used for loan applications in the United States.

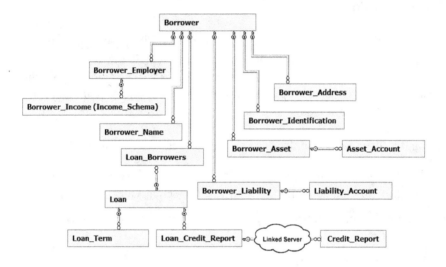

Figure 2-1: Sample **HomeLending** Schema.

The aforementioned database creation script will create tables that are not presented in Figure 2-1. The relationships represented in this schema are specific to the tables that are referenced in this book.

Once the database creation script is executed you can use a data generator tool, such as Red Gate's SQL Data Generator to populate the tables with artificial test data.

Defining Classes of Sensitivity

Our main goal in this study, when considering data classification, is to identify and specify the sensitivity of our data. For example, is it data that is freely and publicly available, or for internal use only, or is it classified information that only certain personnel should be allowed to access?

While here we will restrict ourselves to classification based on data sensitivity only, it's worth noting that such a data classification process will often incorporate further information regarding the management of sensitive data. For example, data classification can be used to manage the data in respect to data retention policies. Among the many regulations that were noted in the prior chapter there are some, such as the United States Department of Health and Human Services' "Health Insurance Portability and Accountability Act" (HIPAA), which defines how long sensitive data is to be retained in addition to identifying its sensitivity.

Disaster recovery planning is another area in which data classification can be useful. In the event of a disaster, the ideal situation is the total recovery of all systems, in a very short timeframe. However, depending upon the nature of the disaster, this is not always possible and so a prioritization of system recovery must be defined. So, for example, the data classification system may assign the following priorities to the various data elements in regard to the urgency of their recovery:

- **Mission-Critical** – a system that must be recovered immediately.

- **Intermediate** – a system that is important, but not critical for the basic functioning of the business.

- **Low** – a subsidiary system that is either disposable, such as a temporary database use to massage data for a special report, or one where limited data loss may be acceptable to the business requiring a less frequent backup schedule.

Data Classification Based on Data Sensitivity

As noted, we'll base our data classification purely on the different levels of sensitivity of the data in our sample database. When defining any data classification system, the definitions of each class must be based upon objective properties that are easily recognizable. The definitions of these classes will reflect the criteria that data must meet in order to be classified to that level. In addition, the definition should include, in general terms, examples of the roles that should have access to data in that class. Clear criteria should be provided that will allow the security analyst to unambiguously recognize the class that should be assigned to an element of data. It may be tempting to suggest methods of mitigating risk with the class descriptions, such as "all data in this class must be encrypted", but this should be reserved for the development of data handling policies which occurs immediately following the creation and assignment of sensitivity classes.

A key aspect to the success of a data classification system, regardless of its purpose, is simplicity. The creation of too many classes will result in a system that is difficult to manage and enforce. In our sample HomeLending database, a simplified scale of sensitivity classes, each presenting a progressive level of severity, will be implemented. The following are the descriptions of our sample class definitions:

- **Low Sensitivity** (General Public)
  Information that is publicly available through other civil sources, or that has been specifically designated as public information by regulation or corporate policy.

- **Medium Sensitivity** (Internal Disclosure Only)
  Information that would cause minor damage to the organization or subject if disclosed externally from the organization. The damage referenced in this description includes exposure to litigation, compromise to security of assets, reputation of organization and its associates, elimination of competitive advantage, and violation of regulation, industry standard or corporate policy. This damage potential will be determined in conjunction with corporate legal counsel. If the class is undeterminable, this is considered the default class.

- **High Sensitivity** (Restricted to Specific Personnel)
  Information that would cause major damage to the organization or subject if disclosed externally from the organization. The damage

referenced in this description includes exposure to litigation, compromise to security of assets, reputation of organization and its associates, elimination of competitive advantage, and violation of regulation, industry standard or corporate policy. This damage potential will be determined in conjunction with corporate legal counsel. This class includes information that is designated explicitly as sensitive or identifiable through regulation, industry standard or corporate policy.

Notice that each class clearly establishes the authorities on which the classification is based. In this case, the classification is based on regulations that are provided by the government, the establishment of industry standards by associated organizations and the internal policies that are established within the company. This provides the analyst with the resources and objectivity needed to implement the classification.

The fact that we have defined the "Medium" sensitivity class as the default, rather than "Low" or "High", instructs the security analyst that the disclosure of all data should be restricted to internal personnel unless otherwise justified.

The definitions of who is permitted to view each level of sensitivity data are intentionally broad at this stage. In the next step of the process, we start to specify the particular groups and individuals that are granted access to this class of data.

Defining Roles According to Classification

In the definition of our sensitivity classes we established, in general terms, which users have access to the data within each class. Within the database, the enforcement of these definitions is handled through **roles**.

It is through roles that the administrator defines and manages permissions to the objects, data and functionality of an installation of the database system, as well as the databases that reside within these systems. Login accounts and users are assigned to roles and are referenced to as "members" of the role. When access to an object, data or functionality is assigned to or revoked from a role it affects all members of that role.

There are two types of roles offered in SQL Server:

- **Server Roles**: This type of role represents a collection of logins at the instance level.

- **Database Roles**: This type of role represents a collection of users at the database level.

SQL Server offers a third type of role that is intended to manage how applications can access databases. It is called the "Application Role". Much like server and database roles, permissions can be granted, revoked and denied to an application role. Unlike server and database roles, members cannot be assigned to an application role. This provides the ability for an application to execute under its own permissions rather than a specific user's permissions.

Access to a database through an application role is accomplished through the passing of a password, from the client application, and the execution of the sp_setapprole system stored procedure, which activates the role. At the point the application role is activated, it supersedes any user accounts that are associated to the login that was used to gain access to the SQL Server instance.

What is the difference between a user and a login account?

Logins are the means by which a connection to a SQL Server **instance** can occur. A login can either be a Windows Login (e.g. MyServer/SmithB), or a SQL Server Login (e.g. sa). Logins are defined at the instance level and do not necessarily represent a specific user. Permissions to instance functionality, such as creating databases, are managed through logins and the server roles of which these logins are members.
Users are accounts that are defined within a specific database and are associated with a login. Permissions to database objects, such as tables and views, are managed through users, and the database roles to which these users belong. A login name and a user name can be the same value.

Creating Database Roles

Using the sample HomeLending database, we will create the database roles that will allow us to manage access to data of varying sensitivity level. These roles will have the role names of Sensitive_high, Sensitive_medium and Sensitive_low, which are based on our simplified sensitivity classes of "High", "Medium" and "Low".

In order to do this, we will use the CREATE ROLE method from SQL Server Management Studio (SSMS). The following is an example of the syntax of this method:

CREATE ROLE [Role Name] **AUTHORIZATION** [Role Owner]

This method's arguments are:

- **Role name**: This is the textual reference to the role. This is used to identify the role when it is in use.

- **Role owner**: This defines who owns the role. The owner can be either a database user or another role.

Defining the role owner argument is optional. If the role owner is not defined, the ownership will be assigned to the database user that created the role. It is the Role Owner that can assign and alter membership of the role.

The script in Listing 2-1 will create the roles in our sample database, according to our sensitivity classes. Please note that in order to successfully execute this script your login account will need to have CREATE ROLE permissions on the database.

```
USE HomeLending;
GO

CREATE ROLE Sensitive_low AUTHORIZATION db_owner;
GO

CREATE ROLE Sensitive_medium AUTHORIZATION db_owner;
GO

CREATE ROLE Sensitive_high AUTHORIZATION db_owner;
GO
```

Listing 2-1: Creating the three sensitivity roles.

45

Creating Logins and Users

Before we can begin assigning members to the new roles, in our sample database, we will need to set up the appropriate server logins and database users. In the HomeLending database will be six database users, each of which will be authenticated to the instance through their respective SQL Server login.

Our first step is to create the SQL Server logins through the use of the CREATE LOGIN method. The following is an example of this method's syntax:

```
-- Creates a SQL Server login
CREATE LOGIN [Login Name] WITH PASSWORD = [Password]

-- Creates a login from a Windows domain account
CREATE LOGIN [Domain Name\Login Name] FROM WINDOWS
```

There are many arguments available for this method. These arguments provide the ability to assign a default schema, default language, default database, the credentials used to access items externally from SQL Server, enforce password expiration policies, and associate the Login with a certificate or asymmetric key from the master database.

When creating a **SQL Server login** the minimum required arguments are:

- **Login Name**: The textual reference to the SQL Server login that is used by the end-user to gain access to the instance.

- **Password**: The textual reference to the password that is used to authenticate the SQL Server login.

When creating a login from a **Windows domain account** (used for Windows Authentication to the instance) the minimum required arguments are:

- **Domain Name\Login Name**: The textual reference to the Windows account, and the domain in which the account exists, that is used by the end-user to gain access to the instance. Please note that the Windows account must exist prior to the creation of the login in SQL Server.

For simplicity, we will be creating SQL Server logins in the instance of our sample database, with the minimum required arguments. The script in Listing 2-2 will create the six SQL Server logins for the instance of our sample database. Please note that in order to successfully execute this script your login account will need to have ALTER LOGIN permissions on the instance.

```
USE HomeLending;
GO

-- Creates SQL Server Logins
CREATE LOGIN SMITHJW WITH PASSWORD = 'as98(*&sssr73x';
GO

CREATE LOGIN JONESBF WITH PASSWORD = 'ghls39**#kjlds';
GO

CREATE LOGIN JOHNSONTE WITH PASSWORD = 'asdpj3$dkEUmwm';
GO

CREATE LOGIN KELLEYWB WITH PASSWORD = 'lkjd&^aslkjdlJD';
GO

CREATE LOGIN REAGANCX WITH PASSWORD = 'HJ777jsb6$@jkjk';
GO

CREATE LOGIN WOLFBA WITH PASSWORD = 'hey4452h#552Vv';
GO
```

Listing 2-2: Creating six SQL Server logins.

Having created the SQL Server logins, we can create the corresponding database users using the CREATE USER method. The following is an example of the syntax of this method:

CREATE USER [User Name] **FOR LOGIN** [Login]

This method's arguments are:

- **User name**: This is the textual reference to the database user name. This is used to identify the database user when it is in use.

- **Login**: This is the textual reference to the login that is to be associated with the user name. If the login is not provided it will map to a login that has the same name as the user account. If a login does not exist an error will be returned.

Additional arguments are available to associate the database user to a certificate or asymmetric key, which will be covered in later chapters. Also, a default schema can be assigned to the database user. The default schema defines the schema within the database that will be searched first for resolving database object names. If the default schema argument is not included, as will be the case in our example, the default "dbo" schema will be used.

Listing 2-3 creates the database users for our sample database. Please note that in order to successfully execute this script your login account will need to have ALTER ANY USER permissions to the database.

```
USE HomeLending;
GO

-- Creates Database Users Mapped to SQL Server Logins
CREATE USER SMITHJW FOR LOGIN SMITHJW;
GO

CREATE USER JONESBF FOR LOGIN JONESBF;
GO

CREATE USER JOHNSONTE FOR LOGIN JOHNSONTE;
GO

CREATE USER KELLEYWB FOR LOGIN KELLEYWB;
GO

CREATE USER REAGANCX FOR LOGIN REAGANCX;
GO

CREATE USER WOLFBA FOR LOGIN WOLFBA;
GO
```

Listing 2-3: Creating the six database users, corresponding to our SQL Server logins.

Assigning Members to Roles

Having created the roles, SQL Server logins and the database users for our sample database, we are now ready to assign membership of each database role. This is accomplished through the execution of the sp_addrolemember system stored procedure. The syntax of this system stored procedure is as follows:

sp_addrolemember [Role Name],[Member Name]

This system stored procedure's arguments are:

- **Role Name**: The textual reference to the database role in which members are being added.

- **Member Name**: The textual reference to the database user, database role, Windows login or Windows group that is being added to the database role specified in the role name argument.

To begin the assignment of members to our roles we will first want to consider the inheritance of our sensitivity classes. All users within the Sensitive_high role are also able to access the items granted to the Sensitive_medium and Sensitive_low roles. All users within the Sensitive_medium role also have access to the items granted to the Sensitive_low role.

Rather than maintaining individual users in all of these roles, we can use the script in Listing 2-4 to implement this inheritance hierarchy. Please note that in order to successfully execute this script your login account will need to have either membership to the db_owner server role or ALTER permissions to the role.

```
USE HomeLending;
GO

-- Sensitive_medium role is a member of Sensitive_low
EXEC sp_addrolemember 'Sensitive_low', 'Sensitive_medium';
GO

-- Sensitive_high role is a member of Sensitive_medium
EXEC sp_addrolemember 'Sensitive_medium', 'Sensitive_high';
GO
```

Listing 2-4: Implementing the inheritance hierarchy in our sensitivity classes.

With this inheritance established, we can now begin to assign the database users to the roles that define their level of access to sensitive data. For our sample database we will assign two database users to each role, as shown in Listing 2-5.

```
USE HomeLending;
GO

-- These users have been determined to have access to low
sensitive data
EXEC sp_addrolemember 'Sensitive_low', 'SMITHJW';
```

```
GO

EXEC sp_addrolemember 'Sensitive_low', 'JONESBF';
GO

-- These users have been determined to have access to
meduim sensitive data
EXEC sp_addrolemember 'Sensitive_medium', 'JOHNSONTE';
GO

EXEC sp_addrolemember 'Sensitive_medium', 'KELLEYWB';
GO

-- These users have been determined to have access to
highly sensitive data
EXEC sp_addrolemember 'Sensitive_high', 'REAGANCX';
GO

EXEC sp_addrolemember 'Sensitive_high', 'WOLFBA';
GO
```

Listing 2-5: Assigning members to the database roles.

Assigning Permissions to Roles

Permissions are used to define who can access specific objects within the database, and the data they contain. Without permissions to a database object, such as a table, view or stored procedure, an end user will not know that the object exists. Permissions can also define how a user interacts with the database object.

There are many defined permissions that allow the security administrator to exert fine-grained control over the objects that a given user or role can access, modify, or execute, and the data that they present. Broadly, we could split these into the following categories:

- **Permissions to allow access to an object and the data it contains**.
  This is also called DML (Data Manipulation Language). For example, granting permissions to execute a stored procedure or user defined function, select data from a table or view, and insert, update and delete data in a table.

- **Permissions to allow management and control of an object and its properties**. This is also called DDL (Data Definition Language). For example, granting permission to create a new object, modify it, or manage permissions of other users or roles to access the object.

While controlling the permissions to all database objects is important for the overall security of the database, our focus is in the protection of sensitive data and so we will be presenting specifically the ANSI-92 permissions that allow control over access to database objects and the data therein.

The ANSI 92 Permissions

The following is a list of permissions that are commonly referred to as ANSI-92 permissions:

- **SELECT** permissions – when granted, allows the user to execute the SELECT queries against a table, view or table-valued user defined function. The SELECT query retrieves rows of data.

- **INSERT** permissions – when granted, allows the user to execute INSERT statements against a table, view or table-valued user defined function in order to add rows of data.

- **UPDATE** permissions – when granted, allows the user to execute UPDATE statements against a table, view or table-valued user defined function in order to change values contained within existing columns of data.

- **DELETE** permissions – when granted, allows the user to execute DELETE statements against a table, view or table-valued user defined function in order to remove rows of data.

- **EXECUTE** permissions – when granted, allows the user to execute a stored procedure or scalar-valued user defined function. If the database objects that are contained within the stored procedure have the identical owner as the stored procedure, the explicit granting of permissions to these underlying database objects are not required. This is known as ownership chaining.

- **REFERENCES** permissions – when granted, allows the user to create a foreign key constraint to a table, view or table-valued user defined function.

51

- **ALL permissions** – when granted, this provides all of the ANSI-92 permissions that are applicable for the given database object. For example, when ALL is granted to a stored procedure only EXECUTE is granted; but when applied to a table DELETE, INSERT, REFERENCES, SELECT and UPDATE are granted.

These permissions can be granted to database users, database roles and server roles by using the GRANT statement in SQL Server Management Studio. The following is an example of the syntax of this statement:

```
GRANT [Permissions] ON [Object] TO [Security Account]
```

This statement's arguments are:

- **Permissions**: The actions the security account can perform. The options for tables, table-valued user defined functions or views are: SELECT INSERT, UPDATE, DELETE and REFERENCES. The options for scalar-valued user defined functions are: EXECUTE and REFERENCES. The only option for a stored procedure is EXECUTE. Alternatively, ALL can be used on any database object to grant the applicable permissions.

- **Object**: The database object to which the permissions are granted. The database objects that can be referenced here are: tables, columns, user defined functions, views, and stored procedures.

- **Security Account**: The reference to the principal that is being granted permissions. The principal can be a Windows Domain Login, Windows Local Login, SQL Server Login, Database User, Database Role or Application Role.

If the implementation of permissions only applies to specific columns within a table or view, a comma separated list of columns must be provided with the object argument. An example of the syntax when assigning permissions to specific columns is as follows:

```
GRANT [Privileges]
    ON [Table/View] ([Column], [Column], [Column]…)
    TO [Security Account]
```

An alternative strategy to assigning permissions on a column-by-column basis is to create a view that contains only the columns that a given user or role is permitted to see, and then to assign permissions to the view, rather than the underlying table. This strategy is covered in detail in Chapter 3.

Occasionally, it may be that while a certain user has been made a member of a role it is deemed that this particular user has no need for a certain privilege that the role has been granted. In cases such as this, the use of the DENY statement in SQL Server Management Studio for this specific user will supersede the permissions defined in their Database Role. The following is an example of the syntax of this statement:

DENY [Privileges] **ON** [Object] **TO** [Security Account]

There may be times when the applied permissions, whether they are granted or denied, must be removed. This is addressed by using the REVOKE statement in SQL Server Management Studio. The following is an example of the syntax of this method:

REVOKE [Privileges] **ON** [Object] **FROM** [Security Account]

In the following chapters there are many examples of the use of GRANT and DENY for the database users for various database objects in the HomeLending database.

Data Definition Permissions

In addition to the ANSI-92 permissions there are privileges that can be granted that extend the user's functionality within the database schema. A few examples of these privileges are as follows:

- Create new objects (CREATE permissions).
- Modify existing objects (ALTER permissions).
- Take ownership of existing objects and maintain permissions to objects. (TAKE OWNERSHIP and CONTROL permissions).
- View the definitions of the database objects (VIEW DEFINITION permissions).

Listing 2-6 shows an example granting the permissions to the Sensitive_high database role to CREATE tables and VIEW DEFINITION of objects in the HomeLending database.

53

```
USE HomeLending;
GO

GRANT CREATE TABLE, VIEW DEFINITION TO Sensitive_high;
GO
```

Listing 2-6: Granting **CREATE TABLE** and **VIEW DEFINITION** permissions to the **Sensitive_high** database role.

These permissions are granted, denied or revoked in the same manner as described for the ANSI-92 permissions.

Evaluating Data for Classification

It is at this step in the process that our understanding of our sensitive data converges with the definition of the sensitivity classes that were defined earlier in this chapter. We are ready to evaluate the data elements in our database and begin assigning them to our sensitivity classes.

The first step is to obtain documentation of all of the fields that are within the database. If captured in a spreadsheet, this overview of each field can provide a convenient way to manage the evaluation and documentation process.

Manually opening each table in SQL Server Management Studio and recording the column information is a mind-numbing, and thankfully unnecessary, experience. There are many excellent third-party tools that can provide documentation of database schemas, such as SQL Doc which is a tool developed by Red Gate Software.

In addition, the INFORMATION_SCHEMA.COLUMNS catalog view will return many properties regarding all of the columns in the database. For our purpose, we are interested only in the schema name, the table name, the column name and the data type of the column, which we can retrieve using the query in Listing 2-7.

```
USE HomeLending;
GO

SELECT
    TABLE_SCHEMA,
    TABLE_NAME,
    COLUMN_NAME,
    DATA_TYPE
FROM
    INFORMATION_SCHEMA.COLUMNS;
GO
```

Listing 2-7: Retrieving column information from the catalog view.

For databases that are in the process of being created, the column information can be gathered from the schema design documentation that is prepared by the Database Architect or Administrator.

As you begin reviewing each of the columns in the database to determine their sensitivity class, consider the following:

- **Your default class**: Earlier in this chapter we discussed the process of defining our sensitivity classes. As a part of the class definition process we defined the class that would be assigned if the sensitivity could not be identified. This is our default class. In the descriptions of our simplified scale of sensitivity classes, used in our sample database, we defined our default class as "Medium". Throughout this process, consider this the assigned class unless otherwise justified and determined.

- **Laws, regulations, standards and policies**: Are there any laws, regulations, industry standards or corporate policies that specifically define the data that is stored in a column as sensitive? If so, consider elevating its sensitivity class. Are there any that specifically define the data stored within the column as public? If so, consider lowering its sensitivity class.

- **Potential damage**: Does the disclosure of the data contained within a column present potential damage to the company or the data subject? If so, consider elevating its sensitivity class.

- **Loss of Confidentiality, Integrity and Accessibility**: Does the disclosure of the data contained within a column present a loss of confidentiality, integrity or availability of the data? If so, consider elevating its sensitivity.

- **Contractual obligations**: Are there any contracts that dictate how the data is to be handled? Some may demand restriction of access while others may demand availability to the public.

The result of this process is documentation that provides valuable information when:

- Implementing methods of access control
- Creating database objects that present a layer of abstraction
- Using the encryption features within the database
- Enforcing sensitive data handling policies.

Using Extended Properties to Document Classification

Each object within a SQL Server database contains a set of properties that define its unique characteristics. Certain properties, such as the date that a table was created, are informational and cannot be changed. However, other properties, such as a column's data type, can be changed and the value assigned to these properties will affect the object's usage.

For our process of establishing and documenting the sensitivity class of each of our columns, it would be useful if there was an informational property available that we could use to record the column's sensitivity class. We could then run a query that would reveal this information on-demand, or we could utilize the property setting programmatically. Unfortunately, SQL Server does not offer such a standard property to define sensitivity. However, we can make use of a feature called **Extended Properties**.

Extended properties allow a custom property to be defined, with a name and a value, for a given database object, which can then be used like a standard property. Extended properties are available on all database objects, including columns in a table.

To view these extended properties through SQL Server Management Studio, simply navigate to the desired object in the Object Explorer, right-click on the object and select the "properties" option. Once the properties window is opened, select the "extended properties" page option, as shown in Figure 2-2.

56

Figure 2-2: Extended Properties Tab in SQL Server Management Studio.

However, for databases with a large number of columns, this method of creating extended property would prove rather tedious. Fortunately, the sp_addextendedproperty system stored procedure provides us a means to accomplish this quickly through a script.

The syntax of this system stored procedure is as follows:

```
sp_addextendedproperty
    @name=[Property Name],
    @value= [Property Value]
    @level0type=[Object type 0],
    @level0name=[Object name 0],
    @level1type=[Object type 1],
    @level1name=[Object name 1],
    @level2type=[Object type 2],
    @level2name=[Object name 2]
```

57

The arguments to this system stored procedure are:

- **Property Name**: The textual reference of the extended property to be created.

- **Property Value**: The value that is to be associated with the new extended property.

- **Object Level**: The object hierarchy that defines the database objects with which the extended property is associated. In our sample database, we are interested in assigning the extended properties to the columns within the tables. The hierarchy for a column is the schema, the table and finally the column itself.

In our HomeLending database, we will execute the script shown in Listing 2-8. This will create the Sensitivity_Class extended property for the Borrower_FName column in the Borrower_Name table, which contains the borrower names. This script will assign the value of "Medium"; thus documenting the column's sensitivity class:

Please note that in order to successfully execute this system stored procedure you will need to have ownership or ALTER or CONTROL permissions to the database objects, in this case a table, in which the extended property is being added.

```
USE HomeLending;
GO

EXEC sp_addextendedproperty
    @name='Sensitivity_Class',
    @value='Medium',
    @level0type='SCHEMA',
    @level0name='dbo',
    @level1type='TABLE',
    @level1name='Borrower_Name',
    @level2type='COLUMN',
    @level2name='Borrower_FName';
GO
```

Listing 2-8: Assigning the medium sensitivity data classification to the Borrower_FName column.

Executing this stored procedure on a per-column basis is probably no quicker than using the navigable features of the Object Explorer in SQL Server Management Studio.

However, armed with the knowledge that our default sensitivity class in our sample database is "Medium", we can construct a query, using the aforementioned catalog view INFORMATION_SCHEMA.COLUMNS catalog view, to assign this sensitivity class to all columns in our database, as shown in Listing 2-9.

```
USE HomeLending;
GO

SELECT
    'exec sp_addextendedproperty ' +
    '@name=''Sensitivity_Class'',' +
    '@value=''Medium'',' +
    '@level0type=''SCHEMA'',' +
    '@level0name=''' + TABLE_SCHEMA + ''',' +
    '@level1type=''TABLE'',' +
    '@level1name=''' + TABLE_NAME + ''',' +
    '@level2type=''COLUMN'',' +
    '@level2name=''' + COLUMN_NAME + ''';'
FROM
    INFORMATION_SCHEMA.COLUMNS;
```

Listing 2-9: Assigning the medium sensitivity data classification to all columns.

This query will produce a complete sp_addextendedproperty statement for each column in the database. We can then copy the results into another query window and execute it to create and assign the default value to all columns.

If a particular column needs to be assigned a higher or lower sensitivity class, then we can manually update the Sensitivity_Class extended property on a case-by-case basis, using either the Object Explorer in SQL Server Management Studio or another system stored procedure, called sp_updateextendedproperty. The arguments of this system stored procedure are identical to the sp_addextendedproperty system stored procedure.

In our HomeLending database, we have a table named Borrower_Identification, which contains the various data that identifies an individual. The Identification_Value column of this table contains the values of social security numbers, driver's license numbers, passport numbers and unique tax payer reference numbers. Based upon our sensitivity class definitions, the column named Identification_Value should be elevated to the "High" sensitivity class. The script shown in Listing 2-10 uses the `sp_updateextendedproperty` system stored procedure to change the value of this extended property from "Medium" to "High":

Please note that in order to successfully execute this system stored procedure you will need to have ownership or ALTER or CONTROL permissions to the database objects, in this case a table, in which the extended property is being updated.

```
USE HomeLending;
GO

EXEC sp_updateextendedproperty
    @name='Sensitivity_Class',
    @value='High',
    @level0type='SCHEMA',
    @level0name='dbo',
    @level1type='TABLE',
    @level1name='Borrower_Identification',
    @level2type='COLUMN',
    @level2name='Identification_Value';
GO
```

Listing 2-10: Raising a sensitivity level using sp_updateextendedproperty.

One of the big benefits of using these extended properties is that we can then use the system metadata function, `fn_listextendedproperty`, to query them. This function is queried in the same way as any table, view or table-valued user defined function.

The syntax of the `fn_listextendedproperty` system metadata function is as follows:

```
SELECT *
FROM
    fn_listextendedproperty
        (
            [Property Name] | default | null,
            [Object type 0] | default | null,
            [Object name 0] | default | null,
            [Object type 1] | default | null,
            [Object name 1] | default | null,
            [Object type 2] | default | null,
            [Object name 2] | default | null
        );
```

The arguments for the `fn_listextendedproperty` system metadata function are:

- **Property Name**: This is the textual reference to the property that is being `queried`.

- **Object Level**: The object hierarchy that defines the database objects with which the extended property is associated. Three levels are required. To return all objects at a given level, use the value "default". Use "null" to ignore a level after the use of "default".

In our `HomeLending` database, we can return the sensitivity class extended property for all columns in the table that store our borrower's asset account numbers, as shown in Listing 2-11.

```
USE HomeLending;
GO

SELECT
    objname as Column_Name,
    name as Extended_Property,
    value as Value
FROM
    fn_listextendedproperty ('Sensitivity_Class',
                             'schema', 'dbo',
                             'table', 'Asset_Account',
                             'column', default);
GO
```

Listing 2-11: Querying extended properties using the `fn_listextendedproperty` system metadata function.

Alternatively, we can query extended properties using the `sys.extended_properties` catalog view. Listing 2-12 shows an example of the syntax of this catalog view:

```
SELECT
        class as Object_Class_ID,
        class_desc as Object_Class_Description,
        major_id as Object_ID,
        minor_id as Column_Parameter_Index_ID,
        name as Extended_Property_Name,
        value as Value
FROM
        sys.extended_properties;
GO
```

Listing 2-12: Querying extended properties using the `sys.extended_properties` catalog view.

Use this catalog view like any other view or table. It can join to other tables and be filtered on any column contained within the catalog view.

Refining the Sensitivity Classes

Although a good start, the classifications in our simplified example are often a little too general to be useful in a real-world commercial business environment. Often the measurements of potential damage to an organization or subject of the sensitive data have more complex levels of measurements than simply "minor" and "major". Also, the internal structure of a commercial business can be rather complex. Simply restricting data to "Internal Use Only" may be a too general and sorely insufficient restriction.

Disclosure Damage Potential

In a real-world scenario, the differentiation of the levels of potential damage to the organization or the subject of the sensitive data can be rather complex. Here is an example of a series of classes that might be more suitable for use in a commercial setting:

Public (General Public) – Information that is publicly available through other civil sources or specifically designated by regulation or corporate policy of its public information status.

Damage Potential: Information that if improperly disclosed presents no exposure to lawsuits, fines, criminal prosecutions, loss of competitive advantage, or loss of consumer confidence.

Private (Internal Personnel Only) – Information restricted in terms of disclosure though regulation or corporate policy.

Damage Potential: Information that if improperly disclosed presents minor exposure to lawsuits, fines, criminal prosecutions, loss of competitive advantage, or loss of consumer confidence.

Confidential (Specific Personnel Only) – This class includes information that is designated explicitly as sensitive or identifiable through regulation, industry standard or corporate policy.

Damage Potential: Information that if improperly disclosed presents significant exposure to lawsuits, fines, criminal prosecutions, loss of competitive advantage, or loss of consumer confidence.

Sensitive (Executive Personnel Only) – This class includes information that is expressly categorized as such by the Chief Executive Officer, Chief Financial Officer, Chief Information Officer or Chief Security Officer of the organization.

Damage Potential: Information that if improperly disclosed presents extreme exposure to lawsuits, fines, criminal prosecutions, loss of competitive advantage, or loss of consumer confidence.

Specialized Cases

In the consideration of sensitivity classes for government and military entities the use of disclosure damage potential is typically the primary delineation of the classes. Below is an example of a series of classes that might be used by a government agency or military:

Unclassified (General Public and Foreign Governments)
Damage Potential: Information that when disclosed has no consequence to national security or military personnel.

Confidential (Military Personnel Only)
Damage Potential: Information that if improperly disclosed presents a threat to national security or military personnel.

Secret (Specific Officials Only)
Damage Potential: Information that if improperly disclosed presents a serious threat to national security or military personnel.

Top Secret (Specific High Level Officials Only)
Damage Potential: Information that if improperly disclosed presents a grave threat to national security or military personnel.

Defining Policies According to Classification

Once the sensitivity classes are defined, the next task is to establish the data handling policies that are appropriate for a given class. These policies help the users of the information determine the usage boundaries for a given class of data, and how Database Administrators are to respond to requests for access to that data.

Any policy must have an owner. This owner is the person who reviews and approves or declines requests for modification to existing policies. They are the ones who coordinate efforts to enforce and audit the compliance to these policies.

As a Database Administrator it is unlikely that you will have this ownership responsibility assigned to you. Typically these policies are owned and defined by the Chief Information Officer or the Chief Security Officer. However, it is still valuable for a DBA to understand this portion of the data classification process.

Information can be used in many ways. These data handling policies must consider how the data may be utilized within the database, and how the data may be transferred and disclosed outside the database. In the latter case, the policies must state the means of disclosure that are permitted for each class, along with any restrictions or procedures that must be applied in each case. For example:

- **Electronic Disclosure**: This covers any electronic transfer of information from the database. It includes presentation of information on a monitor, file transfer protocol (FTP) transmission of information, information passed from a system to another system, presentation of information on the Internet, and information sent through fax, e-mail or texting.

- **Verbal Disclosure**: This covers the disclosure of information from person to person either face-to-face, through the telephone, or public announcement system. Often included in this category is written disclosure that is not sent through the mail.

- **Mail**: This covers disclosure of information through internal and external mailing systems. Special considerations might include the need to add special envelope markings that indicate the sensitivity of the information contained within.

- **Photocopying and Printing**: This covers the act of photocopying and printing information. Unique challenges that are presented in this category might include the need to clear the photocopier or printer cache after use, or the use of a designated printer located in a secure location for printing sensitive documents.

- **Information Storage and Destruction**: The storage and destruction of sensitive data is often subject to regulations that dictate the duration of time it is to be stored. Simply disposing of sensitive information in a dumpster will expose a business to extremely high risk of improper disclosure.

With the sensitivity classes that were used in the HomeLending database we could expect data handling polices that would provide some of the following verbiage:

All data that is categorized with a "High" sensitivity class shall not be displayed in plain text through an application. If presentation through an application is unavoidable the data must be truncated or obfuscated in some fashion to which the data does not present full disclosure.

All data that is categorized with a "High" sensitivity class shall not be transmitted electronically through e-mail, sent to another party through file transfer protocol (FTP), transferred through an interface to another system, published on the internet or other publishing media, sent within a facsimile document. If transfer of this information is required through electronic means, this data must be encrypted with a strong key that is no less than 128 bits in length.

All data that is categorized with a "High" sensitivity class must not be stored in plain text on any data storage device including databases, spreadsheets, documents, backup files and flat files. The storage of this data must either be truncated or encrypted with a strong key that is no less than 128 bits in length. The storage and retention period of this data must be in compliance with government regulations, industry standards and corporate policies.

All data that is categorized with a "Medium" or "High" sensitivity class must not be stored on a portable device, such as a thumb drive, CD, DVD or hard drive within a laptop, in plain text. If storage on a portable device is required, this data must either be truncated or encrypted with a strong key that is no less than 128 bits in length.

All data that is categorized with a "Medium" or "High" sensitivity class shall not be provided in plain text on printed reports or documents. If printing is required, this data must be truncated or obfuscated in such a fashion that the plain text no longer presents a security threat.

Summary

With our sensitivity classes defined, our database roles established, members assigned to the roles, our data handling policies defined, and having evaluated the data within our database and documented it, we are now ready to take a look at how our database schema may need to be designed, or re-architected, to protect our sensitive data.

Chapter 3: Schema Architecture Strategies

Policies define how we are to interact with sensitive data. Classification helps us recognize sensitive data and allow us to apply the policies and database security features. We now turn our attention to the physical structure in which data is stored and organized. This is known as the schema architecture.

The design of the schema architecture contributes heavily to the database's storage efficiency, performance, scalability and integrity through a process called normalization. Normalization can also improve the protection of sensitive data through the physical separation from non-sensitive data. In addition, the utilization of database object schemas, views and linked servers can further enhance this separation resulting in a very effective level of abstraction that will enhance your sensitive data protection efforts.

In this chapter we will cover more specifically how normalization, database schema objects, views and linked servers can be utilized to further the protection of sensitive data.

Overview of HomeLending Schema Architecture

Before we begin the dive into the details of the various schema design strategies that we'll use to protect sensitive data in the HomeLending database, it's worth taking a "big picture" look at the schema design that we plan to implement, as shown in Figure 3-1.

This figure illustrates three of the four design strategies that we'll cover in this chapter:

1. The third normal form level of normalization that is applied to the schema architecture of the HomeLending database.

2. The introduction of the Income_Schema database object schema, to house the sensitive Borrower_Income table, and its relationship to the tables in the default database object schema (dbo).

3. The implementation of a linked server for the Credit_Report data.

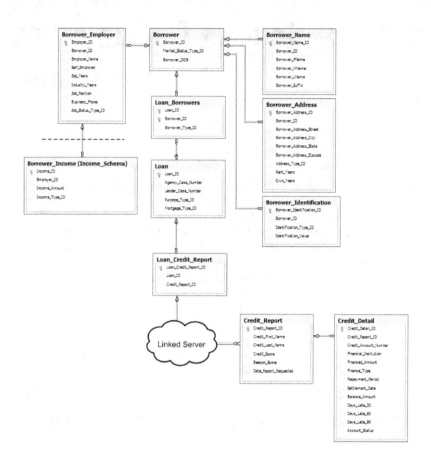

Figure 3-1: Portion of the HomeLending schema that will be presented in this chapter.

It is worth noting, in regard to the introduction of the Income_Schema database object schema, that in reality we would probably extend this concept, for example creating a "Borrower" database object schema for the borrower tables rather than have all the remaining tables in the dbo schema. However, we've kept things relatively simple here in order to better illustrate the concepts in this book.

The fourth strand of our strategy, not depicted in Figure 3-1, is the abstraction of the database schema, using views, in order to simplify data queries for the end user and also prevent them from viewing unauthorized data.

Protection via Normalization

Defining the storage structure of data is an important step in the creation
of a database. The process of breaking up a mass "lump" of data into
logical and relational collections is called **normalization**. This process
defines the organization of tables, their relationship to other tables, and the
columns contained within the tables. The proper and appropriate application
of normalization is a critical component in ensuring the integrity and
confidentiality of the data.

The degree to which normalization has been applied is measured primarily by
levels of "normal form". These levels are defined by specific criteria that must
be met by the schema design. Each of these levels is cumulative. The higher
form cannot be achieved without first meeting the criteria of the lower forms.
Since the introduction of relational databases there have been many forms of
normalization developed; but the three most common forms of normalization
are first normal form, second normal form and third normal form. Among
these common forms, the separation of data into logical groups that is possible
through third normal form provides the highest level of protection of sensitive
data. Figure 3-2 shows a de-normalized version of `Borrower` information that
resides in our `HomeLending` database.

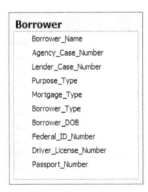

Figure 3-2: De-normalized example of borrower tables.

The criteria that define the three most common levels of normal form are
described in the following sections. In practice, the level of normalization that
is targeted may vary depending upon the intended use of the tables. A table that
contains data that will be modified regularly, such as in an on-line transaction
processing database (OLTP), will benefit from a higher level of normalization,

due to the reduction in redundant data storage within the database. A table that contains data that is static, but heavily read, such as an on-line analytic processing database (OLAP), will benefit from a lower level of normalization due to the reduction of joins required to access related data.

First Normal Form

- Data should be separated into tables, each of which contains columns that are logically similar.

- Each of these tables should have a unique identifier, known as a primary key, which represents each row and prevents duplicate rows.

- The columns in the table should not contain any "repeating groups" of data.

Figure 3-3 shows a version of the borrower information that meets the criteria for first normal form. The loan data is stored in a separate table from the borrower information. A single borrower record can be related to multiple loan records. Each record contains its own primary key and the data is not repeated across the data row.

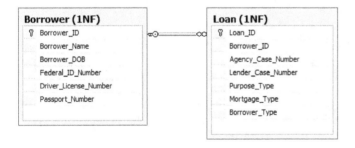

Figure 3-3: First normal form example of borrower tables.

Second Normal Form

- The non-primary key columns that are contained within the table must be dependent upon the primary key. If the data in the table applies to multiple rows within the table it should be moved to a separate table.

- Tables contain values that are related to other tables' primary key. These values are called foreign keys.

70

Figure 3-4 shows a design for the borrower information that meets the criteria for second normal form. Notice that the `Borrower_Type`, `Purpose_Type` and `Mortgage_Type` columns have `_ID` added to their names. These items are now foreign keys to reference tables. Also, the introduction of the `Loan_ Borrowers` table allows many borrowers to be related to many loans. The movement of the borrower type to the `Loan_Borrowers` table allows for each borrower relationship to loans to be defined individually.

Figure 3-4: Second normal form example of borrower tables.

Third Normal Form

- Table data only contains data that is dependent upon the primary key.

Figure 3-5 shows a design for the borrower information that meets the criteria for third normal form. The borrower's federal id number, driver's license and passport number are pulled into a `Borrower_Idenitification` table, as the combination of `Identification_Type_ID` and `Identification_ Value` columns. We will see the benefits of this change later in this book when we discuss encryption. Additionally, the borrower name is pulled out of the borrower table, allowing multiple versions of names for a borrower such as alias and maiden names. The names have also been broken out to their respective parts for more flexible usage.

71

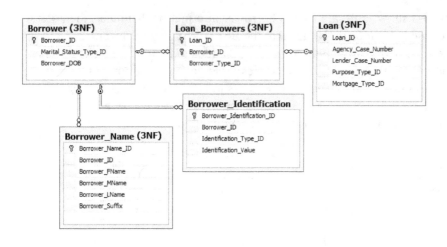

Figure 3-5: Third normal form example of borrower tables.

Normalization and Data Redundancy

When a database is well normalized, the occurrence of repeating information throughout the database is reduced or eliminated. This, in turn, reduces or eliminates the likelihood that data is updated in one place and not another, thereby introducing inconsistencies. Consider, for example, a store that sells T-shirts. This store may have many types of shirts in their inventory, from many suppliers. If their database was not normalized they would likely have the supplier's address in each row of their inventory. When a supplier notifies them of a change of address they would need to update every row that contained the old address. This difficult task will be made worse by the fact that it is probable that the address was recorded inconsistently throughout the database, and so it's likely that some instances will be missed.

If their database was normalized, the address information for each supplier would be maintained in a single location in the database, most likely in a "supplier address" table, related to the supplier table. This would result in consistency in the address information, elimination of the need to continually enter the address information, and would make the address change process a snap.

Normalization and Data Security

For security purposes, the reduction in data redundancy provides an environment that can be managed in a more effective manner. Furthermore, the separation of sensitive information from identifying information reduces the value of the sensitive information to the potential data thief, and provides a degree of obscurity to the casual, yet authorized, viewer.

Consider the following example from our HomeLending database, illustrated in Figure 3-6. The Borrower table has a one-to-many relationship to the Borrower_Employer table. This design lets us capture each employer that the borrower lists on their application. The borrower's income data is stored in a separate table, called Borrower_Income, and is related to the Borrower_Employer table.

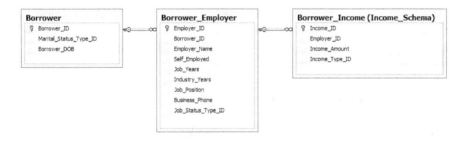

Figure 3-6: Borrower table to Borrower_Income table relationship.

As a DBA you might find yourself, one fine day, troubleshooting the Borrower_Income table in this database. The table is opened and within it is income information for all borrowers. Since the table has been effectively normalized, the only data that is disclosed will be a series of rows containing money values, each associated with a numeric foreign key, referring to the Borrower_Employee table. If the table were not normalized, it is likely that each piece of income data in the table would have the borrower's name next to it, disclosing confidential and identifying data. In addition, you could make a fair bet that the borrower's federal tax identification number would be there too!

Normalization and the Borrower_Identification table

Let's now take a look at the `Borrower_Identification` table, depicted in Figure 3-7, and consider its use of normalization.

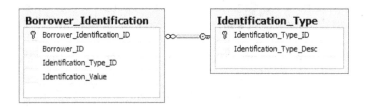

Figure 3-7: The `Borrower_Identification` table.

This table's design is unique in that the `Identification_Value` column is used to store various values that are used to validate identity, such as federal identification number, passport number and driver's license number. The `Identification_Type_ID` column is a foreign key to a reference table called `Identification_Type`. It is the `Identification_Type_ID` column that differentiates these values for each row.

An example of the data that would be contained within the `Borrower_Identification` table is shown in Table 3-1.

Borrower_ ID	Identification_ Type_ID	Identification_Value
103	2	R7KFU413243TDDIN
103	1	555-08-4862
103	3	6311791792GBR6819855M297028731

Table 3-1: Sample data from the `Borrower_Identification` table.

One benefit of this column reuse is flexibility. This design allows quick implementation of new forms of identification validation; it simply involves creating a new record in the `Identification_Type_ID` column.

Another benefit to column reuse is the obscurity that this approach introduces to the column's data. If the contents of this table were disclosed, the viewer would still need to gain additional information, in this case the contents of the Identification_Type table, as well as the contents of the Borrower table, in order to make the disclosure useful for fraudulent purposes.

Separating sensitive data from the object to which it relates, using normalization, is a fundamental security strategy. However, we can go even further than that. A single SQL Server installation, also known as an instance, can hold up to 32,767 databases. We can strategically place blocks of sensitive data in their own databases to provide a layer of obscurity and separation that extends to the physical data files, transaction logs and back up files.

Querying data across multiple databases within an instance of SQL Server requires the use of the fully qualified object names, as demonstrated by the query in Listing 3-1.

```
SELECT
    bnam.Last_Name,
    ident.Identification_Value
FROM
    Database1.dbo.Borrower bor
        INNER JOIN Database1.dbo.Borrower_Name bnam
      ON bor.Borrower_ID = bnam.Borrower_ID
    INNER JOIN Database2.dbo.Borrower_Identification bi
      ON bor.Borrower_ID = bi.Borrower_ID;
GO
```

Listing 3-1: Qualifying object names in cross-database queries.

Please note that the HomeLending database schema does not reflect the specific cross database architecture shown in Listing 3-1. It is offered only as an example of this approach.

Using Database Object Schemas

Throughout this chapter the word "schema" has been used as a general term to describe the database architecture and its objects. However, in SQL Server the term schema, or more formally **Database Object Schema**, refers to the namespace, or container, in which database objects reside. Inside the database object schemas are database objects, such as tables, views and stored procedures, which can be grouped together logically. This offers a way to organize your database objects and control access to them at a group level.

75

When a user is denied access to a database object schema, they cannot view or access any of the database objects within it. This offers a level of obscurity to portions of the overall database schema design and can be used to separate highly sensitive data from less sensitive data. Figure 3-8 illustrates how a user may have access to one database object schema, in this case the default database object schema of dbo, while being denied to all objects within another database object schema, here, the Income_Schema database object schema.

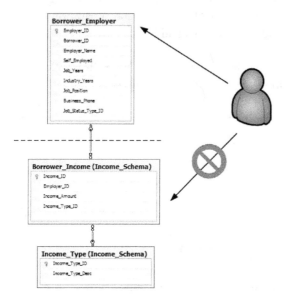

Figure 3-8: A user with permissions to the default database object schema while being denied access to the Income_Schema database object schema.

Database object schemas offer an effective method of protecting sensitive data through separation, and can also make permission management less of a headache to the DBA. To create a database object schema in a database the CREATE SCHEMA method will be executed in SQL Server Management Studio. The following is an example of the syntax of this method:

```
CREATE SCHEMA [Schema Name] AUTHORIZATION [Schema Owner]
```

This method's arguments are:

- **Schema name**: This is the textual reference to the database object schema.

- **Authorization**: This is the textual reference to the schema owner. This argument is optional. When this argument is not included the user creating the database object schema is set as the object owner.

In the HomeLending database, the only role that we want to allow to modify database objects, or set permissions, in the Income_Schema schema is the Database Role of db_owner. Therefore, the statement that was used to create the Income_Schema schema includes the AUTHORIZATION argument, as shown in Listing 3-2.

```
Use HomeLending;
GO

CREATE SCHEMA [Income_Schema] AUTHORIZATION [db_owner];
GO
```

Listing 3-2: Creating the **Income_Schema** database object schema.

Having created the database object schema, we can use the GRANT, DENY and REVOKE statements to manage permissions to that schema, in a similar fashion to the manner in which we've previously used them to manage permissions to database objects.

An example of the syntax used to grant SELECT, INSERT and UPDATE privileges to the Sensitive_high Database Role for the Income_Schema database object schema, is shown in Listing 3-3.

```
Use HomeLending;
GO

GRANT SELECT, INSERT, UPDATE
        ON SCHEMA::Income_Schema
        TO Sensitive_high;
GO
```

Listing 3-3: Granting permission to select, insert and update data in **Income_Schema** to the **Sensitive_high** database role.

Notice the two colons (::) used in reference to the schema. This is a scope qualifier. A scope qualifier defines that the permissions are restricted to a specific object type. In this case, we defined the object type to be a schema and then reference the schema on which we wish to grant permissions.

When referencing database objects, it is good practice to refer to them with their fully qualified name, which will include a reference to the database object schema in which the object resides. When the database object schema is not included, SQL Server will search the database user's default database object schema to try to find the database object that is being referenced; if the database object is not found an error will be returned stating that the object is invalid.

Listing 3-4 shows a sample query in which the fully qualified names of the tables in the default database object schema, which is dbo, and the Income_Schema schema, are referenced.

```
Use HomeLending;
GO

SELECT
    be.Employer_Name,
    bi.Income_Amount,
    it.Income_Type_Desc
FROM
    dbo.Borrower_Employer be
    INNER JOIN Income_Schema.Borrower_Income bi
        ON be.Employer_ID = bi.Employer_ID
    INNER JOIN Income_Schema.Income_Type it
        ON bi.Income_Type_ID = it.Income_Type_ID;
GO
```

Listing 3-4: Using fully qualified database object names.

Using Views

Views are objects within SQL Server that provide a layer of abstraction between the end users and the underlying schema. Rather than directly access the base table, the users query a "virtualized table" that holds only the data that is specific to their needs.

Users can execute SELECT statements against a view in the same way that they would if they were querying the underlying tables. If the query that is used to create the view is an updateable query, in other words, one that references a single base table and does not present aggregated data, then UPDATE, INSERT and DELETE statements can also be executed against the view. It is worth noting that executing an INSERT statement against a view that does not contain all of the underlying table's columns will result in an error if the columns that are not included in the view do not allow nulls and do not have a default value.

This abstraction of the database schema, using views, means that data can be represented in a more friendly way to the end user. The query that defines the view can perform any required aggregation of the data, thus saving the user from having to perform complex joins, summing, grouping and filtering to return the required data. Views are often used to report sales and to identify trends to which management needs to respond.

Views also have an important security function. As well as providing a useful reporting mechanism for end users, they provide a mechanism by which to prevent those end users viewing any data that their role does not have authorization to access. If a user had direct access to a table, say our Credit_ Report table, which contained a mix of low and high sensitivity columns then it would be difficult to prevent the user from viewing the high-sensitivity items. Instead, we can create a view that exposes only the low-sensitivity columns and give the role permission to query that view, rather than the underlying table, as illustrated in Figure 3-9.

Therefore, through a view, the security administrator can allow users access to the aggregated data they need for reporting, while obscuring the structure of the schema and reducing the risk of accidental or intentional disclosure of sensitive data.

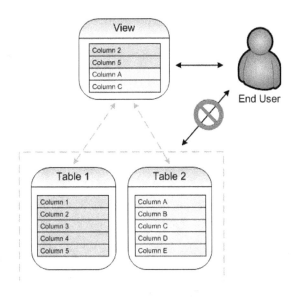

Figure 3-9: Illustration of a view.

Creating Views

Views can be created by using the CREATE VIEW method. The following is an example of the syntax of this method:

CREATE VIEW [View Name] **AS** [Select Statement]

This method's arguments are:

- **View Name**: The textual reference to the view. This should include the schema in which the view belongs.

- **Select Statement**: The select statement that is executed to present the data in the view.

In our sample database, we will create a view as shown in Listing 3-5, which will present the basic borrower information without revealing any sensitive data:

```
Use HomeLending;
GO

CREATE VIEW [dbo].[vwBorrower]
AS
SELECT
    b.Borrower_ID,
    ba.Borrower_Address_Street,
    ba.Borrower_Address_City,
    ba.Borrower_Address_State,
    ba.Borrower_Address_Zipcode,
    at.Address_Type_Desc,
    bn.Borrower_LName,
    bn.Borrower_MName,
    bn.Borrower_FName
FROM
    dbo.Borrower b
    INNER JOIN dbo.Borrower_Address ba
    ON b.Borrower_ID = ba.Borrower_ID
    INNER JOIN dbo.Borrower_Name bn
    ON b.Borrower_ID = bn.Borrower_ID
    INNER JOIN dbo.Address_Type at
    ON ba.Address_Type_ID = at.Address_Type_ID;
GO
```

Listing 3-5: Creating a view in the HomeLending database.

Once the view is created we can assign permissions to the view.

Assigning Permissions to Views

In Chapter 2 of this book we explored data classification. As a result of that process, we created some Database Roles and added some SQL Server Logins as members. These roles were designed to manage the permissions to database objects; therefore controlling the disclosure of sensitive data.

In our sample database, we have utilized views to abstract the architecture of our schema. We will not grant the Database Roles permission to access the table objects. If a user, other than the database owner, were to access the database through SQL Server Management Studio and try to view the table objects, none would appear. Instead, we will grant permission to access only the view objects. When stored procedures and user defined functions are created they too will have the appropriate permissions granted to them.

In Listing 2-9 of Chapter 2, we used extended properties to assign a sensitivity of "medium" to all columns in our database. Therefore, the columns used in our view, named vwBorrower, contain data that is classified as "medium" and so we will need to grant permissions to access this view to the Database Role named Sensitive_medium.

For data integrity purposes, we do not want users deleting records. Also, the vwBorrower view is not updatable since it contains joins to other tables; therefore, only the SELECT privileges are granted, as shown in Listing 3-6.

```
Use HomeLending;
GO

GRANT SELECT
    ON dbo.vwBorrower
    TO Sensitive_medium;
GO
```

Listing 3-6: Granting to the database role, Sensitive_medium, permission to select on the view vwBorrower.

Since the Database Role named Sensitive_high is included as a member of the Sensitive_medium Database Role, we do not need to explicitly grant permissions to the Sensitive_high Database Role.

At this point, every login that is a member of the Sensitive_meduim or Sensitive_high role will have permission to access our view. However, let's say we have a specific user, with a SQL Server Login of JOHNSONTE, who meets the overall requirements for membership of the Sensitive_medium role but should be restricted to specific data due to other policies. In this case, the internal policy dictates that JOHNSONTE should not have access to details regarding a borrower's loan history.

To deny the SQL Server Login JOHNSONTE of SELECT privileges to the vwBorrower view, the command shown in Listing 3-7 would be executed.

```
Use HomeLending;
GO

DENY SELECT
        ON dbo.vwBorrower
        TO JOHNSONTE;
GO
```

Listing 3-7: Denying SELECT privileges to the SQL Server login JOHNSONTE.

At some point during the course of business, the previous internal policy has been changed and this user is now allowed access to loan data. To remove the previous DENY that was implemented we will use the REVOKE command. This command removes any previously granted or denied permissions. The use of the REVOKE command is illustrated in Listing 3-8:

```
Use HomeLending;
GO

REVOKE SELECT
        ON dbo.vwBorrower
        FROM JOHNSONTE;
GO
```

Listing 3-8: Returning SELECT privileges to JOHNSONTE.

The result of this action removes the restriction to that view and his login is now consistent with the other members of the Sensitive_medium Database Role.

Harnessing Linked Servers

Linked Servers offer to security administrators, when implementing their schema architecture strategies, an additional layer of separation between sensitive and less sensitive data. Often, certain pieces of sensitive data are required by several different applications or departments within an organization. However, rather than store this data in multiple places, with the attendant security risk that this entails, it may be desirable to store the data in one place only, on a separate physical server, to which access can be strictly regulated. This server may be in a separate geographic location from the servers that contain information of lower sensitivity.

So, for example, rather than having a customer's federal tax identification number stored in multiple systems, with "varying" levels of security applied in each case, you can place it on a central server that can be securely accessed by all systems that need this information. This "centralized" architecture has several advantages:

- It ensures that the data is consistently protected and that its access is easily managed.

- It reduces the redundancy of sensitive data throughout the enterprise

- It provides benefits for disaster recovery due to the ability for a linked server to reside in a separate physical location.

- It provides a separation in the administration responsibilities, which reduces the risk of the DBA being the source of disclosure.

Access to the SQL Server instance containing the sensitive data, from other servers in the system, is enabled using **Linked Servers**.

NOTE:

While it's optimal that the linked instance resides on a separate physical server, it can also reside on the same physical server in another SQL Server instance.

This feature of SQL Server allows commands from one instance of SQL Server to be executed against another instance through an OLE DB (Object Linking Embedding Database) provider, as shown in Figure 3-10.

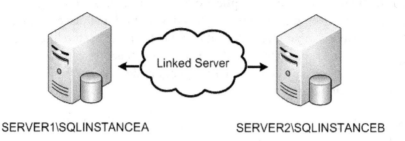

SERVER1\SQLINSTANCEA   SERVER2\SQLINSTANCEB

Figure 3-10: Linked servers.

The linked server does not necessarily need to house a SQL Server instance. There are OLE DB providers that allow you to link to an Oracle database, DB2, XML, or MS Access, and various other database platforms are supported through Open Database Connectivity (ODBC) drivers.

Implementing Linked Servers

In our sample HomeLending database, we will use a linked server to access credit report data for our borrowers. Rather than storing the credit report details, which are packed with account numbers, balances, and federal tax identification numbers, alongside the loan application data, they will be stored in a separate physical server (Server2), with highly restricted access, as shown in Figure 3-11.

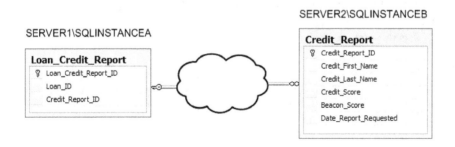

Figure 3-11: Foreign key to a table on a linked server.

We'll allow only the interface with the credit bureau to write data and the users that gain access to this linked server will be carefully defined and granted only read permissions. Therefore, through the use of linked servers the credit report details in our sample database are stored securely in a server that is dedicated to that sensitive data. Its reference to any borrower information that would be identifiable is through a foreign key that is stored in our primary server, referenced in Figure 3-11 as `SERVER1\SQLINSTANCEA`.

Linked servers are implemented using the `sp_addlinkedserver` system stored procedure, the syntax of which is as follows:

```
sp_addlinkedserver  [Server Name],[Product Name],
                    [Provider Name],[Data Source],
                    [Location],[Provider String],
                    [Catalog]
```

This system stored procedure's arguments are as follows:

- **`Server Name`**: The textual reference to the linked server that is being added. If using the native SQL Server OLE DB provider the server and instance name of the target database is the value that should be entered.

- **`Product Name`**: A descriptor of the database product that is being connected. For example: "SQL Server" or "Oracle".

- **`Provider Name`**: The unique programmatic identifier of the OLE DB provider that is being used. This can be obtained using the provider name value from the results of executing the extended stored procedure `xp_enum_oledb_providers`. If this argument is omitted, it will default to the native SQL Server OLE DB provider.

- **`Data Source`**: The textual reference to the instance that is accessed through the linked server. The value of this argument is dependent upon the provider used. If the native SQL Server OLD DB provider is used this argument should be omitted. This argument is passed as a property to the OLE DB provider.

- **`Location`**: The textual reference to the location of the linked server database. This argument is passed as a property to the OLE DB provider.

- **`Provider String`**: The textual reference to the connection string to the instance that is being linked. This argument is passed as a property to the OLE DB provider.

- **Catalog**: The textual reference to the specific database that is being accessed through the linked server. This argument is passed as a property to the OLE DB provider.

Not all of the arguments are applicable to all OLE DB providers. In the case of the native SQL Server OLE DB provider, simply providing the server name and product is sufficient.

Once a linked server has been created, its logins will need to be established to provide access to it. This is accomplished by executing the sp_ addlinkedsrvlogin system stored procedure, the syntax of which is as follows:

```
sp_addlinkedsrvlogin [Linked Server Name],[Use Self],
                     [Local Login],[Remote User],
                     [Remote Password]
```

This system stored procedure's arguments are:

- **Remote Server Name**: The textual reference to the linked server for which the login is being created.

- **Use Self**: A value of true indicates that the users connect to the linked server using the credentials that are used on the primary server. A value of false indicates that the credentials that are used to login to the linked server are different than the credentials used to login to the primary server.

- **Local Login**: The SQL Login or Windows Login that is used to gain access to the linked server.

- **Remote User**: The SQL Login used to gain access to the linked server, if the Use Self argument is set to false.

- **Remote Password**: The password used to gain access to the linked server if the Use Self argument is set to false. Please note that this argument is passed to the linked server in plain text.

- For the benefit of the HomeLending database, which resides on SERVER1\SQLINSTANCEA, we will create a linked server, referenced as SERVER2\SQLINSTANCEB, using the native SQL Server OLE DB provider, in which the credit report data will be stored. The server login on the linked server will be the same as that used on our primary server, as shown in Listing 3-9.

```
USE Master;
GO

EXEC dbo.sp_addlinkedserver
    @server = N'SERVER2\SQLINSTANCEB',
    @srvproduct=N'SQL Server';
GO

EXEC dbo.sp_addlinkedsrvlogin
    @rmtsrvname=N'SERVER2\SQLINSTANCEB',
    @useself=N'True',
    @locallogin=NULL,
    @rmtuser=NULL,
    @rmtpassword=NULL;
GO
```

Listing 3-9: Implementing a linked server.

You may notice that the script used to create the linked server reference is
executed on the Master database on our primary server rather than the
HomeLending database. This is due to the fact that a linked server is a server
object, rather than a database object, which can be available to any database
that is created within the primary server.

Querying Linked Servers

In order to query the data contained on a linked server you must include the
server name and instance name in the fully qualified name of each database
object. If the OLE DB data source is a database other than SQL Server you will
need to consider any syntax differentiation when writing queries against that
data source. Listing 3-10 shows a sample of a query in which the credit report
data is being combined with the loan application data in our sample database.

```
Use HomeLending;
GO

SELECT
    ln.Lender_Case_Number,
    cr.Credit_Score,
    cr.Beacon_Score,
    cr.Date_Report_Requested
FROM
    dbo.Loan ln
    INNER JOIN dbo.Loan_Credit_Report lncr
        ON ln.Loan_ID = lncr.Loan_ID
```

87

```
        INNER JOIN [SERVER2\SQLINSTANCEB].CreditReport
                        .dbo.Credit_Report cr
           ON lncr.Credit_Report_ID = cr.Credit_Report_ID;
  GO
```

Listing 3-10: Query the Linked Server.

Network Security

There are some additional security considerations when implementing linked servers as a means of protecting sensitive information. Data will be traveling across network lines and potentially across the Internet. Performance will be affected but, more importantly given our security focus, it will also introduce a potential vulnerability to data being gleaned through hackers monitoring network traffic.

The encryption features of SQL Server are designed to protect data at rest, which is the data while it is in storage. Once the data is queried and decrypted it is considered data in transit and the protection of the data is dependent upon other security measures on the network such as Secure Sockets Layer (SSL). If the data that is stored on a linked server is encrypted, the encryption and decryption processes will likely occur at the linked server; otherwise the script in Listing 3-10 will need to include the commands for cryptographic functions. More details in regard to these cryptographic functions will be discussed in the coming chapters.

Summary

The methods that are presented in this chapter do not suggest that obscurity and abstraction alone are sufficient methods to protect sensitive data. Implementing methods of obscurity in concert with additional methods of obfuscation, encryption and access management provide a more complex and secure environment than implementing any single method.

CHAPTER 4: ENCRYPTION BASICS FOR SQL SERVER

The hieroglyphic messages that are inscribed upon the walls of the tombs of the Egyptian Pharaohs were a mystery for many centuries. Through the ages there were many attempts to translate these images, but none were wholly successful until the discovery of the Rosetta Stone in 1799. This stone was engraved with three versions of the same message; one in hieroglyphic, one in Egyptian demotic, and one in Greek. It provided the key required to deciphering these ancient images.

In the context of data security, the Rosetta Stone is analogous to the cryptographic key that is used to transform, or *encrypt*, data into unreadable text called *cipher text*, and then to *decrypt* it back into a readable format called *plain text*.

The practice of encrypting and decrypting data is known as cryptography, and is a common and effective method of protecting sensitive data. SQL Server provides many cryptography features such as cell-level encryption and Transparent Data Encryption (TDE) to protect data at rest. Secure socket layers (SSL) and transport layer security (TLS) for message transmission as well as WiFi Protected Access (WPA) for wireless communications are just a few examples of the use of cryptography in protecting data in transit.

In this chapter, we will explore the keys that are used to perform cryptographic functions in SQL Server, and their relationship to each other within the key hierarchy. We will also explore the maintenance considerations in regard to these keys that will ensure that they provide a consistent and enduring level of protection, and are always securely backed up. It is through these maintenance processes, and more expressly through the backup of encryption keys, that you will avoid the dreaded "lost key" scenario.

We'll explore the different types of key algorithm that can be used to encrypt the keys and data in our database, and introduce the built-in cryptographic functions that implement these algorithms in SQL Server. Finally, we'll review some of the SQL Server catalog views that we can interrogate to obtain values metadata regarding our keys and encrypted data. These functions and views are used extensively throughout the book, and reference information regarding their syntax and usage can be found in Appendix A.

Cryptographic Keys

The main character on the cryptographic stage is the key. A key contains the algorithm, the sequences of instructions which is used in the various cryptographic functions that SQL Server provides to encrypt and decrypt data.

An encryption function uses the key to describe how the plain text will be converted into cipher text. Likewise, without the key, the decryption process cannot occur.

Many types of keys are available to work with the cryptography features and functions of SQL Server, arranged into a distinct hierarchy.

Cryptographic Key Hierarchy

The keys that are used with the cryptography features of SQL Server are structured in a layered, or hierarchical, composition. Each layer of keys encrypts the underlying layer of keys and ultimately the data itself, as shown in Figure 4-1.

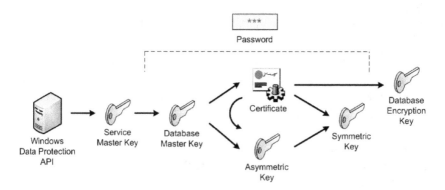

Figure 4-1: Encryption Key Hierarchy.

This hierarchy provides a highly secure infrastructure for sensitive data. At the top of the hierarchy is the service master key, which operates at the SQL Server Instance level and is used to protect the database master keys, in each database. This renders the database useless outside of its instance. In addition, without the use of the service master key to protect the database master key, the database master key must be explicitly opened prior to its use.

The database master key is used to encrypt the private keys for asymmetric keys and certificates within a database. By applying this level of protection these private keys cannot be decrypted outside of the database unless the database master key is also provided.

Asymmetric keys and certificates are used to protect the other private keys, symmetric keys and data contained within the database. The symmetric keys within the database are used to protect other symmetric keys as well as data within the database. This inner dependency provides a level of security that is much more resistant to unauthorized access.

Service Master Key

The Service Master Key is encrypted using the machine key from the Windows Data Protection API (DPAPI), using the password of the Windows Service Account credentials of the server in which the SQL Server instance is installed.

When an instance of SQL Server is installed, and its service is started for the first time, the service master key is created. There can be only one service master key per instance.

The catalog view sys.symmetric_keys can be used to verify the service master key's existence, as shown in Listing 4-1. The service master key is identified with the name ##MS_ServiceMasterKey##.

```
USE master;
GO

SELECT * FROM SYS.SYMMETRIC_KEYS;
GO
```

Listing 4-1: Querying the symmetric_keys catalog view for the service master key.

91

The service master key is often used to provide protection to other keys within a database. It is also a critical component of the Transparent Data Encryption (TDE) feature of SQL Server 2008.

Database Master Key

This key is unique to each database within the SQL Server instance. If an item is encrypted using the database master key, it cannot be decrypted outside of that database. The database master key is not automatically generated when a database is created, instead it is created using the CREATE MASTER KEY command, as shown in Listing 4-2.

```
Use HomeLending;
GO

CREATE MASTER KEY ENCRYPTION BY PASSWORD = 'MyStr0ngP@
ssw0rd2009';
GO
```

Listing 4-2: Creating a database master key in the HomeLending database.

You can verify the existence of the database master key by querying the sys.symmetric_keys catalog view, using either the master database or the database for which the database master key was created. The database master key is identified with the name ##MS_DatabaseMasterKey##.

A database master key can be used to protect the asymmetric keys, certificates, as well as sensitive data, contained within the database. The database master key is protected through the use of the service master key and/or a password.

Asymmetric Key

Asymmetric keys consist of a public key, which is distributed to selected individuals, and a private key to which access remains highly restricted. In SQL Server, the public key can decrypt data that has been encrypted by a private key and vice-versa.

Asymmetric keys can be created within a database through the execution of the CREATE ASYMMETRIC KEY command.

```
Use HomeLending;
GO

CREATE ASYMMETRIC KEY MyAsymKey
    WITH ALGORITHM = RSA_2048
    ENCRYPTION BY PASSWORD = 'MyStr0ngP@ssw0rd2009';
GO
```

Listing 4-3: Creating an asymmetric key in the HomeLending database.

Again, you can query **sys.asymmetric_keys** to verify that the asymmetric key was successfully created.

Asymmetric keys are used to protect other keys within the database, as well as sensitive data. This type of key is highly resource intensive and, when used to protect sensitive data, it should be used with smaller data sets or messages.

Certificates

A certificate is used in much the same way as an asymmetric key in that it involves a public/private key pair. The primary difference is that a certificate private key is digitally associated with an individual or device whereas the asymmetric key is not. The industry standard known as the Internet X.509 Private Key Infrastructure (PKI) defines the contents and signature requirements for a valid certificate, and certificate private key.

In SQL Server, a certificate's private key can either be imported from an external assembly, or generated within the database. In the latter case, this is called a *self-signed certificate*. The certificate private key that is generated within SQL Server is in compliance with the PKI standard.

Listing 4-4 demonstrates the creation of a certificate can be created within a database using the CREATE CERTIFICATE command.

```
Use HomeLending;
GO

CREATE CERTIFICATE MySelfSignedCert
    ENCRYPTION BY PASSWORD = 'MyStr0ngP@ssw0rd2009'
    WITH SUBJECT = 'Self Signed Certificate',
    EXPIRY_DATE = '05/31/2010';
GO
```

Listing 4-4: Creating a certificate in the HomeLending database.

93

Once again, you can query `sys.asymmetric_keys` to verify the existence of the certificate in the database in which you attempted to create it.

When creating a certificate, you can specify arguments that define its activation date (`START_DATE`) and expiration date (`EXPIRY_DATE`). These properties can be used in the management of a certificate's lifecycle. SQL Server does not enforce the activation and expiry dates that are associated with a certificate. Additional logic, or the use of the Extensible Key Management (EKM) feature of SQL Server, must be employed to enforce these dates.

Certificates are used to protect other keys within the database as well as sensitive data.

Symmetric Key

When an item is encrypted using a symmetric key it must be decrypted using that same key. The service master key, database master keys and database encryption keys are all examples of symmetric keys. Additional symmetric keys can be created within a database using the `CREATE SYMMETRIC KEY` command, as shown in Listing 4-5.

```
Use HomeLending;
GO

CREATE SYMMETRIC KEY MySymKey
    WITH ALGORITHM = AES_256
    ENCRYPTION BY PASSWORD = 'MyStr0ngP@ssw0rd2009';
GO
```

Listing 4-5: Creating a symmetric key in the HomeLending database.

Querying `sys.symmetric_keys`, in the context of the database in which the symmetric key was generated, will verify that the symmetric key was successfully created.

Symmetric keys are used to protect other keys within the database as well as sensitive data. Symmetric keys can be protected by other symmetric keys, asymmetric keys, certificates and passwords.

Database Encryption Key

The database encryption key was introduced in SQL Server 2008. This key is specifically designed to support the Transparent Data Encryption (TDE) feature of that product. The purpose of this key is to perform the encryption/decryption process on the physical files and file groups of the database.

The database encryption key is located in the user database while the asymmetric key, or a certificate, that protects the database encryption key resides in the master database. This is not only necessary to decrypt the key that protects the physical files of the database; but also provides the "transparent" opening of the database encryption key and cryptographic functionality without the requirement of additional coding to manage it.

Database encryption keys can be created within a database through the execution of the CREATE DATABASE ENCRYPTION KEY command. Due to this key's exclusive use by the Transparent Data Encryption feature of SQL Server 2008, the specifics of creating and using a database encryption key will be covered in more detail in Chapter 6.

Passwords

In this day and age the concept of a password is one that is widely understood. These are the strings of characters used to login to computer systems, check our e-mail, activate household security systems and access voicemail messages. In SQL Server, passwords are an option that is available to protect other keys within a database. For example, the use of a symmetric key requires it to be opened prior to its reference in cryptographic processes. If a symmetric key is protected by a password, the string of characters that consists of the protecting password must be passed for it to be opened.

Passwords are defined with an argument to the key's respective CREATE commands. Each of the keys covered in this chapter, with the exception of the service master key, include the ENCRYPTION BY PASSWORD argument in their creation script examples.

An alternative to using passwords to protect the keys within the database is the use of symmetric keys, asymmetric keys or certificates. Password protecting keys improve the portability of keys since they are not dependent upon items that are database or instance specific; although, this portability does allow the protected item to be restored to another instance and compromised to reveal its contents therefore reducing its level of security.

Key Maintenance

Cryptographic keys and passwords that protect keys are not a "set-it-and-forget-it" feature of securing sensitive data; they require periodic maintenance to ensure that the items that are protected remain at their highest level of security. Regular maintenance of keys and passwords reduces the occurrences of the patterns of encryption being discovered through the monitoring of encrypted values, a practice called crypto-analysis. It reduces the occurrences of key fatigue, in which bits of plain text begin to appear among the cipher text. In the unfortunate situation when a key is revealed, improperly disclosed or lost, the scope of the compromised data is reduced if the entire body of sensitive data is not protected with the same key.

This maintenance is handled by shepherding each key through a lifecycle, illustrated in Figure 4-2, which defines when a key is created, used for the first time in encryption and decryption, expired for encryption purposes, retired from use and finally eliminated.

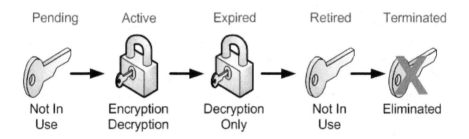

| Pending | Active | Expired | Retired | Terminated |
| Not In Use | Encryption Decryption | Decryption Only | Not In Use | Eliminated |

Figure 4-2: Key lifecycle.

Other than providing a means to create new keys and regenerate encrypted data with a new key, SQL Server does not offer a built-in means to manage keys through this lifecycle. At first glance, this may seem to be a bad oversight but, in fact, provision of key management functionality within the database that contains the encrypted data and keys introduces a potential vulnerability in data security.

Extensible Key Management (SQL Server 2008)

To address the maintenance issue, SQL Server 2008 introduced functionality called Extensible Key Management (EKM).Through the *Microsoft Cryptographic API* (MCAPI) provider, this feature offers the ability to implement a third party solution, or even a custom built solution, for generating, backing up, exporting, distributing, retrieving keys and managing the overall key lifecycle externally from the database. EKM also enables use of devices such as *Hardware Security Modules* (HSM), smartcards, and fingerprint readers to store, configure and manage key lifecycles.

MCAPI cryptographic providers can be created in SQL Server through the execution of the CREATE CRYPTOGRAPHIC PROVIDER command, as shown in Listing 4-6. The .dll file provided in this example represents a third party product that would be used for key management functionality.

```
Use Master;
GO

CREATE CRYPTOGRAPHIC PROVIDER MyCryptoProvider
    FROM FILE = 'D:\InstanceA\CryptoProvider\CryptA.dll';
GO
```

Listing 4-6: Creating a cryptographic provider in SQL Server.

You can query sys.cryptographic_providers to verify that the provider was successfully created.

The use of EKM, by default, is disabled. To begin to use this feature of SQL Server you will need to first execute the script in Listing 4-7.

```
sp_configure 'show advanced',1;
GO
RECONFIGURE
GO

sp_configure 'EKM provider enabled',1;
GO
RECONFIGURE
GO
```

Listing 4-7: Enabling EKM.

Once the cryptographic providers have been created and EKM is enabled these keys can be utilized to perform encryption and decryption of other keys and data through the standard built-in cryptographic functions that are provided with SQL Server.

Backing up Keys

Whenever the topic of encryption is being discussed there is a question that inevitably arises. This question is in regard to how encrypted data can be recovered if the key is lost or corrupted. The answer is a short one: the data will be lost. That is unless you have backed up all of the keys that are used in the encryption effort.

When the database is backed up through the built-in SQL Server database back up process, some keys are included in the back up file and others are not. The asymmetric keys and symmetric keys that are created within the database, as well as the database encryption key that is used in the TDE feature, are all included in the database backup. The service master key, database master key and certificates are not included in the database backup. Each of these keys must be backed up as a separate task, using the following commands:

- **BACKUP SERVICE MASTER KEY**

- **BACKUP MASTER KEY**

- **BACKUP CERTIFICATE**

Each of these commands contains an ENCRYPTED BY PASSWORD option which protects the backup files with the defined password, as shown in Listing 4-8.

To recover these keys, knowledge of this password is required.

```
Use master;
GO

-- backup service master key
BACKUP SERVICE MASTER KEY TO FILE = 'D:\InstanceA\Backup\
SMK.bak'
    ENCRYPTION BY PASSWORD = 'MyB@ckUpP@ssw0rd';
GO

Use HomeLending;
GO
```

```
-- backup database master key
BACKUP MASTER KEY TO FILE = 'D:\HomeLending\Backup\DMK.bak'
    ENCRYPTION BY PASSWORD = 'MyB@ckUpP@ssw0rd';
GO


-- backup certificate
BACKUP CERTIFICATE MySelfSignedCert
   TO FILE = 'D:\HomeLending\Backup\MySelfSignedCert.bak'
   WITH PRIVATE KEY (
            DECRYPTION BY PASSWORD = 'MyStr0ngP@
ssw0rd2009',
   FILE = 'D:\HomeLending\Backup\MySelfSignedCert.pvk',
            ENCRYPTION BY PASSWORD = 'MyB@ckUpP@
ssw0rd');
GO
```

Listing 4-8: Backing up the service master key, database master key and certificate.

It is highly recommended that these key backup files are stored on separate media from the database backup files so that, in the event that the media that contains the database backup files is stolen or compromised, the data contained within the database remains secured. The decryption of the data and files contained in the backup media would require access to the backup media that contained the key backup files.

Key Algorithms

Keys use a set of instructions that dictate how their cryptographic functions are to be performed. These instructions are called algorithms. There are several algorithms available in SQL Server and selecting the optimal algorithm can be a daunting task, with the high complexity of the mathematical equations that define these algorithms simply adding to the challenge. Each encryption project is unique and a suitable algorithm for one project may not be suitable for another. With the following information you can more confidently select the algorithm that is best for your situation.

Symmetric Key Algorithms

The available symmetric key algorithms in SQL Server fall into two categories:

- **`Block ciphers`**: This type of algorithm processes a fixed number of bits of the plain text into the same fixed number of bits of encrypted text. Decryption of a block cipher reverses the process.

- **`Stream ciphers`**: This type of algorithm processes a single bit of plain text into a single bit of cipher text and the results have a keystream, which is a series of bits that provides the key to the encryption, appended to its results.

Depending upon the algorithm selected, the resulting block or stream cipher is a key of a specific length. In general, the longer key lengths result in stronger encryption; although stronger encryption means more resources when it is processed.

The following key algorithms are available for symmetric keys in SQL Server:

Advanced Encryption Standard

- **`AES 128`**: This is a block cipher that processes text in 128 bit blocks. The result is a key size of 128 bits.

- **`AES 192`**: This is a block cipher that processes text in 128 bit blocks. The result is a key size of 192 bits.

- **`AES 256`**: This is a block cipher that processes text in 128 bit blocks. The result is a key size of 256 bits.

Data Encryption Standard

- **`DES`**: This is a block cipher that processes text in 64 bit blocks. The result is a key size of 56 bits.

- **`DESX`**: This option in SQL Server is actually a misnomer and when it is used, `Triple_DES_3KEY` is actually applied. The **`DESX`** option will not be an option in future versions of SQL Server.

- **`Triple_DES`**: This is a block cipher that processes text in 64 bit blocks. The result is a key size of 168 bits. The `Triple_DES` option in SQL Server actually returns a 128 bit key size. The `Triple_DES_3KEY` option returns a 192 bit key size. `Triple_DES` is the algorithm used when a database master key is created.

Rivest Cipher

- **RC2**: This is a block cipher that processes text in 64 bit blocks. The result is a key size of 64 bits.

- **RC4**: This is a stream cipher resulting in a key size between 40-256 bits. This option will be removed from future versions of SQL Server.

- **128-bit RC4**: This is a stream cipher resulting in a key size of 128 bits. This will not be an option in future versions of SQL Server.

Of the three options, AES, DES and RC, the AES group of algorithms is the strongest. This is reflected in the fact that the US National Security Agency states that the AES algorithm should be used to protect systems and information of national security interest.

Due to the inherent weaknesses of the RC4 and 128-bit RC4 algorithms these options will not be available in future versions of SQL Server. Their use is therefore discouraged.

Asymmetric Key Algorithms

Asymmetric keys utilize a series of computational methods to derive the private and public key instead of the block/stream methods identified for symmetric keys. The following **Rivest/Shamir/Adleman (RSA)** key algorithms are available for asymmetric keys in SQL Server:

- **RSA 512**: The result is a private key size of 512 bits.

- **RSA 1024**: The result is a private key size of 1024 bits.

- **RSA 2048**: The result is a private key size of 2048 bits.

When a self-signed certificate is generated within SQL Server, the private key that is created uses the RSA 1024 algorithm.

It is important to note that the term "key length" for asymmetric keys is in reference to the portion of the algorithm calculation that is called the "modulus"; whereas the key length for symmetric keys is the resulting block or stream cipher. The physical storage size of a key that uses the RSA 512 algorithm is actually 64 bits. This can be a source of confusion when comparing the key lengths of symmetric and asymmetric keys.

Asymmetric algorithms are, in general, stronger than symmetric algorithms; but they are significantly more resource intensive.

Due to the key length of the RSA 512 algorithm, which is 512 bits, it is not considered suitable for protecting highly sensitive data.

In addition to encryption, the RSA algorithms are also used as a method of digitally signing messages. Message signing is the process in which the original message is encrypted with a private key and attached to the plain text message. When the message is received, the message is encrypted again through the use of a public key. The two hash values are then compared. If they are a match, it is verification that the message has not been altered during transit and verifies that the sender is authentic.

Hashing Algorithms

Hashing is a process in which plain text is encrypted without the intent of it being decrypted. The revelation of the plain text value occurs when a string is encrypted with the same algorithm and returns a positive match. This is also known as one-way encryption.

The following key algorithms are available for hashing functions in SQL Server:

Message Digest

- **MD2**: The result is a 128 bit hash.
- **MD4**: The result is a 128 bit hash.
- **MD5**: The result is a 128 bit hash.

Secure Hash Algorithm

- **SHA**: The result is a 160 bit hash.
- **SHA1**: The result is a 160 bit hash.

Both offerings within the Secure Hash Algorithm (SHA) series utilize the same base algorithm to determine its hash value; but the SHA1 option contains an extra step in its processing to address a security flaw discovered in SHA option.

With the hash length of the SHA being greater than the MD options, the former are considered to be the more secure.

The `SignByAsymKey` and `VerifySignedByAsymKey` cryptographic functions of SQL Server utilize the `MD5` algorithm when signing plain text with an asymmetric key.

Built-In Cryptographic Functions

A function is a database object that contains a block of code that can be referenced in a command to return either a single value, in which case it is called a scalar function, or a set of data, in which case it is called a rowset function. For example, calling the `GETDATE()` scalar function will return the current date.

SQL Server offers many built-in functions that can be used for aggregation, mathematical calculations, date and time handling, text and string handling and the execution of security tasks. In the interest of securing sensitive data, we will be focusing on those functions that address cryptographic functionality, which are:

- **AsymKey_ID**
- **Cert_ID**
- **CertProperty**
- **DecryptByKeyAutoAsymKey**
- **DecryptByKeyAutoCert**
- **EncryptByAsymKey** and **DecryptByAsymKey**
- **EncryptByCert** and **DecryptByCert**
- **EncryptByKey** and **DecryptByKey**
- **EncryptByPassPhrase** and **DecryptByPassPhrase**
- **Key_ID**
- **Key_GUID**
- **SignByAsymKey**
- **SignByCert**
- **VerifySignedByAsymKey**
- **VerifySignedByCert**

Starting in the very next chapter, and throughout the book, we'll be using several of these built-in cryptographic functions to perform tasks such as the following:

- Transformation of plain text to cipher text (encryption).

- Transformation of cipher text to plain text (decryption).

- Obtaining of a key's id by passing its name.

- Verification of an asymmetric key or certificate's signature.

- Return of a certificate property.

For reference information regarding the syntax and usage of each of these functions, please refer to Appendix A. The ability to execute these built-in functions will depend upon the user's ownership or permissions to the object that it is referencing. For example, if the user does not have ownership or permissions granted to a certificate, they will not be able to encrypt data, decrypt data or return the certificate's properties through these built-in functions.

Encryption Catalog Views

Catalog views are a valuable tool in SQL Server, through which the metadata information of a database or an instance can be queried.

While all users in the PUBLIC server role have permissions to query catalog views, the results of the queries can differ based upon the user's ownership and permissions to the objects to which the metadata refers. If ownership or permissions are not granted to the user performing the query, the metadata for that object will not be returned.

Various categories of Catalog view are available, allowing you to query metadata for CLR assemblies, extended properties, schemas, linked servers and security, to name just a few. In the interest of securing sensitive data, we will use, in the coming chapters, some of the catalog views that fall in the security category and that are specific to encryption, which include:

- **Sys.Asymmetric_Keys**

- **Sys.Certificates**

- **Sys.Credentials**

- **Sys.Crypt_Properties**

- **Sys.Cryptographic_Providers**

- **Sys.Key_Encryptions**

- **Sys.OpenKeys**

- **Sys.Symmetric_Keys**

For reference information regarding the syntax and usage of each of these views, please refer to Appendix A. These catalog views can be queried, after creating their associated objects, as a means of verifying that the execution was successful, or for gleaning valuable information that can be used elsewhere in the application, such as a certificate's expiration date.

Generally, these catalog views will be used in conjunction with the EXISTS command to determine if the item already exists in the database. This information can then be used to direct the execution of CREATE and ALTER commands, accordingly. Listing 4-9 shows an example of using a catalog view in this manner:

```
USE HomeLending;
GO

IF NOT EXISTS
    (
    SELECT * FROM SYS.ASYMMETRIC_KEYS
    WHERE NAME = 'MyASymKey'
    )
    BEGIN
        --[CREATE ASYMMETRIC KEY COMMAND HERE]--
    END;
GO
```

Listing 4-9: Checking for the existence of a key.

Summary

Through this chapter you have gained a basic understanding of the keys used in the encryption process, the hierarchy used in establishing a layered approach to protecting the keys, the understanding that keys should be maintained to ensure their effectiveness and the algorithms available in SQL Server to generate the keys.

In the following chapters of this book we will explore the details of implementing and using cell-level encryption, Transparent Data Encryption and hashing methods; all of which utilize these keys and functions. Specific examples will be illustrated in context of our sample HomeLending database.

CHAPTER 5: CELL-LEVEL ENCRYPTION

Honeybees collect nectar from various plants and flowers throughout the landscape and carry it to their hives, in which the nectar is converted into honey and placed into many hexagonal-shaped cells. Each cell within the hive is protected with a layer of wax. When the honey is harvested by the beekeeper, this layer of wax is removed, exposing the honey.

Much like a beehive, a data table consists of many cells. Each of these cells are grouped and organized in rows and columns. The "sealing wax" for each cell is the cell-level encryption that protects its contents.

In this chapter we will explore those fundamentals of cell-level encryption that must be understood prior to its use. We will also walk through an example that implements a column-level approach to cell-level encryption, using the HomeLending database, in which the permissions to encrypt and decrypt the value contained in a column are granted only to the Sensitive_high database role.

We will also define and create the interface, composed of a view and two stored procedures, through which users will interact with our encrypted data.

As we approach the world of cell-level encryption, it is important to note the value and strength of this option. We also should consider that those items that are fantastic in moderation are often less than spectacular in abundance. Cell-level encryption can be an expensive data protection option. As noted later in this chapter, this option requires careful planning and strategic use in order to reduce its performance impact.

Not all sensitive data requires the granularity and strength that cell-level encryption offers. Consideration and utilization of other protection methods, covered in later chapters, in concert with cell-level encryption, are the secret to achieving the right balance between security and performance.

Granularity of Cell-level Encryption

At cell-level, encryption's finest level of granularity, each cell that contains encrypted data is protected by a key that is specific to the user that performed the encryption. Decryption is accomplished through the use of the same key, or a public key, depending on the encryption method applied.

At this level of granularity, the user is presented, in plain text, with only the data elements on which they have been granted decryption permissions, as depicted in Figure 5-1.

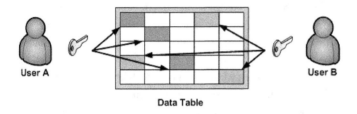

Data Table

Figure 5-1: Cell-Level Encryption Granularity.

Alternatively and more commonly, one can apply cell-level encryption at a less granular level, encrypting all cells within a single column with the same key. Permissions to decrypt with this key would then be granted to members of a database role.

The level of granularity that is used is entirely dependent upon the requirements dictated by the data classification process, its surrounding policies and the fine balance between security and performance.

Benefits and Disadvantages of Cell-Level Encryption

Cell-level encryption is a valuable tool in the tool belt of the Database Administrator; but much like the hammer in the carpenter's tool belt, it is not suited to all situations. The following review of cell-level encryption's benefits and disadvantages will provide some aid in the determination of whether this approach is best suited for your situation.

The benefits of cell-level encryption include:

- **Granular** – encryption can be provided at a much finer-grained level than the entire database. It offers the means to encrypt a single cell within the table uniquely from another cell.

- **Secure** – the element of data that is encrypted remains in that state, even when recalled into memory, until it is actively decrypted.

- **User Specific** – users can be granted access to keys that encrypt and decrypt data that is exclusive to their use.

The disadvantages of cell-level encryption include:

- **Data type restrictions** – implementation of cell-level encryption requires schema modifications. All encrypted data must be stored with the `varbinary` data type.

- **Expensive table scans** – due to the nature in which the values are encrypted any referential constraints, primary keys and indexes on data that is encrypted is no longer used. This results in table scans when encrypted data is referenced in queries.

- **Processing overhead** – the additional processing required for encrypting and decrypting data has a cost to the overall performance of the database.

The use of cell-level encryption does present its own unique set of challenges and costs; but these should not dissuade from the consideration of its use.

The actual performance impact of cell-level encryption will vary depending upon the environment in which the database resides. The size of the impact that cell-level encryption has on the database performance will depend on the server's hardware, such as load balancing, number of processors and amount of available memory, as well as on non-hardware items such as query optimization, index placement and overall database design.

In the `HomeLending` database, we took advantage of normalization to isolate our sensitive data. It is only accessible, through a view, to a select number of users that perform decryption. Also, it is through a stored procedure, which also is available to a very limited number of users, that the encryption functions are executed. Thus, the performance impact is much less than if it were available to all users of the database, or if the column remained in a high-traffic table. When cell-level encryption is strategically implemented, it is a very effective method of protecting sensitive data at the highest degree of granularity.

Special Considerations

The consideration of the benefits and disadvantages of cell-level encryption is important in the decision to select this method to protect sensitive data. Additionally, there are also some special considerations that are worthy of note:

Searching Encrypted Data

It is not uncommon for an application to allow authorized users to retrieve information regarding an individual, based upon a query that uses sensitive data in its search condition. An example would be a system that recalls a customer by their Social Security Number or Tax Identification Number.

This scenario presents a paradox that confounds protection efforts of sensitive data. On one hand, the business requirements demand the ability to recall individuals through identifiable data. On the other hand, granting the ability to pass plain text into queries presents a very high risk of disclosing sensitive data to unauthorized users who are monitoring database activity.

One approach might be to first decrypt the data that is stored in the database and then compare the plain text to the plain text that is passed in the WHERE clause. However, this approach does not provide a solution to the passing of sensitive data as plain text into the query and it will have a *severe* impact on the performance of the query, for the following reasons:

- The query must perform the decryption for all rows in the table, one-by-one, in order to determine a match.
- Indexes will not be used, so the query execution will result in a table scan.

An alternative approach would be to encrypt the plain text, using the same process that generated the cipher text that is stored in the column, before it is passed into the WHERE clause of the query.

While this may overcome the security issue of passing the plain text value into the query, it would not provide the expected results. This is due to the fact that when cipher text is generated through an encryption method in SQL Server, a **salt** is appended.

A salt is a series of random characters that are added to the plain text prior to its encryption. In this way, a unique hash is created each time the plain text is encrypted. This provides protection from the cipher text being revealed through the observance of its patterns. As a result, the query will never return a match, even with the underlying plain text being identical.

If efficient searchability, as well as security of the sensitive data, is required then cell-level encryption will not be the solution for the data in question. In this case one-way encryption, which will be discussed in more detail in Chapter 7, should be considered as an alternative.

Encrypting Large Plain Text Values

Documents and manuscripts may contain information that would be classified at a high sensitivity level. The plain text size of these items can often be very lengthy. The challenge that this type of data presents is that all of the cryptographic functions for symmetric and asymmetric keys in SQL Server return a varbinary type with a maximum length of 8,000 bytes. This translates to a maximum plain text length, for encryption, of 7,943 characters.

When the plain text length exceeds this upper limit, the encryption method returns a NULL value, so the encryption not only fails but you also lose the data you were trying to encrypt.

In order to get round this limitation, and use cell-level encryption for large plain text documents, one option is to chop the data into smaller units. For example, the manuscript can be encrypted in segments according to natural breaks that occur in the document, such as chapters. However, this approach would require additional schema modifications since these separate units will require relational storage for efficient retrieval.

Another option is to investigate whether or not the large text really does require encryption because the intent to obfuscate data does not necessarily call for encryption. As an alternative, consider converting the plain text directly into a varbinary data type with a length designation of max, using the CONVERT method. An example of this syntax is:

```
CONVERT(Varbinary(max),@YourPlainText)
```

111

The `max` length designation increases the storage limit from a maximum of 8,000 bytes to 2,147,483,647 bytes. Assuming that the plain text length is within this size this statement will return a `varbinary` version of the plain text that is equal to the full length of the string.

Its resulting value is not discernable to the naked eye. To return this value to plain text requires only the conversion of the `varbinary(max)` data to a `varchar(max)` data type using the same `CONVERT` method. This approach does not provide the same security level as that offered by cell-level encryption, but it does overcome the data type size limitations associated with the cryptographic functions, and it may suffice if a limited degree of obfuscation is required.

Preparing for Cell-Level Encryption

Using the `HomeLending` database, we will implement cell-level encryption. For simplicity and clarity we will focus on the `Borrower_Identification` table. The majority of the steps noted in this demonstration would be repeated as needed for each column in any table that contains data classified as "High" sensitivity.

Before we begin, we will need to examine our database and generate the requirements that will guide our approach to implementing cell-level encryption.

Reviewing the Borrower_Identification Table

The `Borrower_Identification` table contains references to a borrower's various forms of identification, such as Security Number, Driver's License Number and Unique Tax Identification Number.

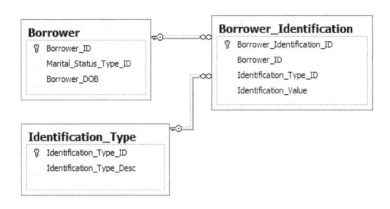

Figure 5-2: Borrower_Identification table.

The columns defined in this table are as follows:

- **Borrower_Identification_ID**: The primary key, containing an integer value that uniquely identifies each row.
  Sensitivity class: medium, due to our defined default class.

- **Borrower_ID**: An integer value; this is the foreign key, relating to rows contained within the `Borrower` table.
  Sensitivity class: medium, due to our defined default class.

- **Identification_Type_ID**: This integer value identifies the type of identification that is stored in the `Identification_Value` column. Through this foreign key to the `Identification_Type` table the verbose reference of the identification type, such as "Social Security Number" can be obtained.
  Sensitivity class: medium, due to our defined default class.

- **Identification_Value**: This variable character value contains the plain text representation of the actual identification value. For example, if the identification type was a Social Security Number the value contained in this column would be something like "555-55-5555".
  Sensitivity class: high.

Through the grouping of logically similar columns, the use of a unique row identifier, the absence of repeating columns, the use of foreign keys and the fact that the columns contained within this table are dependent only upon the primary key, we can see that this table has achieved third normal form.

This level of normalization has provided a separation of this sensitive data from data that is classified with a lesser level of sensitivity. It also confers the benefits of our first requirement:

Requirement 1: Permission to Modify Sensitive Data

The only individuals that will update or insert data into tables containing high sensitivity columns will be members of the Sensitive_high database role.

The normalization that has been achieved for the Borrower_Identification table is representative of the other tables that have been created throughout the HomeLending database.

Database Object Access Control

Direct access to all tables within the HomeLending database has been denied to the members of the Sensitive_high, Sensitive_medium and Sensitive_low database roles. An example of the script that was used on the Borrower_Identification table is shown in Listing 5-1:

```
USE HomeLending;
GO

DENY ALTER,CONTROL,REFERENCES,DELETE,INSERT,UPDATE,SELECT
    ON dbo.Borrower_Identification
    TO Sensitive_high, Sensitive_medium, Sensitive_low
GO
```

Listing 5-1: Denying access to the base tables.

Views and stored procedures will be developed that provide the means by which our users will interact with these tables. By implementing this structure we can control the access to our data at a more granular level than simply granting access to entire tables. In addition, this architecture affords us the opportunity to embed cryptographic functionality, and other logical methods, into objects such as views and stored procedures.

This provides us with our second requirement:

Requirement 2: Access to Base Tables

All users will be denied access to all base tables. Access to data will be mediated through the use of views and stored procedures.

Key Encryption and Performance

Performance is king when it comes to databases. When transaction volumes are extremely high, performance is elevated to an even higher level of importance and security of sensitive data often takes a back seat. Indeed, there is a cost to implementing encryption. However, our goal within the `HomeLending` database is to implement cell-level encryption in such a way that it has minimal impact on performance.

Asymmetric key encryption is based on a complex algorithm and provides a very high level of protection. However, with this complexity comes a commensurately high processing cost.

The strength of symmetric key encryption is dependent upon the length of the keys that are used. The lengthier keys provide a higher level of security but, again, come with a higher processing cost. Symmetric key algorithms are in general less complex and therefore weaker than those for asymmetric keys, which results in faster processing.

When dealing with large volumes of data and transactions, the tremendous affect asymmetric keys have on performance is often too high a price to pay for the stronger encryption that they provide. Therefore, we arrive at our third requirement:

Requirement 3: Encryption Algorithms

All High sensitivity data will be protected with a symmetric key that utilizes the AES algorithm. This results in a key length of 128 bits, which is consistent with specifications defined by regulations, industry standards and corporate policies.

Determining the Key Hierarchy

In SQL Server, the use of symmetric key encryption requires that the key be opened prior to use. Once a key is opened it remains open until the database connection is terminated or it is explicitly closed. Leaving a key open for the duration of a session does provide a level of convenience, but also introduces a degree of vulnerability to "hacking." As such, it is recommended that you explicitly close keys as soon as you have finished using them.

Symmetric keys are protected by other keys, certificates or a password. This prevents the unauthorized use of a key to encrypt and decrypt sensitive data. This also presents a challenge when implementing and maintaining the related code that uses the keys.

If a key is protected by a password, the stored procedures that use the OPEN SYMMETRIC KEY method would either have to:

- Obtain the password from another source
- Have the password hard-coded into the code
- Require the password to be passed as an argument to the stored procedure.

Obtaining the password from another source would require additional resources that could negatively affect the performance of our cryptography functionality. The hard-coding of passwords presents a maintenance nightmare, as well as security concerns regarding plain text passwords being embedded in our code. A hacker who is tracing database activity will be able to intercept a plain text password that is being sent as an argument to a stored procedure. If the password is passed as a hashed value, that too adds additional resources.

Our understanding of the encryption key hierarchy, discussed in the previous chapter, will help us overcome this challenge. The service master key, which was automatically generated when our instance was installed, can be used to protect a database master key. A database master key can be used to protect a self-signed certificate, which in turn can be used to protect our symmetric key. This hierarchy not only provides a seamless and maintainable structure, but it also reduces the possibility that the sensitive data can be disclosed externally from the database and instance.

Therefore, we arrive at our fourth requirement:

Requirement 4: The Encryption Key Hierarchy

All symmetric keys that are used to protect sensitive data will utilize the encryption key hierarchy and be protected by a self-signed certificate that is secured by the database master key. The database master key will be protected by the service master key.

Implementing Cell-Level Encryption

We are now ready to begin the implementation of our cell-level encryption, based on our previous requirements. This involves two basic steps:

- Implementing and testing the chosen key hierarchy.
- Modifying the schema to store the encrypted data.

Implementing the Key Hierarchy

We will implement our key hierarchy based upon requirements 3 and 4. The service master key is the highest tier in this hierarchy and exists at the instance level. As previously noted, the service master key of our instance was created when our instance was setup. The pre-existence of the service master key can be confirmed by querying the sys.symmetric_keys catalog view of the master database for the key with the name of ##MS_ ServiceMasterKey##, as shown in Listing 5-2.

```
USE master;
GO

SELECT
    *
FROM
    sys.symmetric_keys
WHERE
    name = '##MS_ServiceMasterKey##';
GO
```

Listing 5-2: Confirming the existence of the Service Master Key.

Our first step will be to create a database master key for our HomeLending database. This is accomplished using the CREATE MASTER KEY method. The ENCRYPTION BY PASSWORD argument is required and defines the password used to encrypt the key, as shown in Listing 5-3.

```
USE HomeLending;
GO

CREATE MASTER KEY
    ENCRYPTION BY PASSWORD = 'MyStr0ngP@ssw0rd2009';
GO
```

Listing 5-3: Creating the Database Master Key.

The requirement of defining the ENCRYPTION BY PASSWORD argument might be a bit confusing since our intent, based upon requirement 4, is to protect the database master key with the service master key, instead of a password. Creating the database master key, as shown in Listing 5-3, not only protects the database master key with a password; but also automatically adds the additional protection by the service master key. The use of either key encryption method is valid for opening the database master key.

If we execute a query against the sys.key_encryptions catalog view, for the ##MS_DatabaseMasterKey## key , as shown in Listing 5-4, we see that ENCRYPTION BY MASTER KEY is returned, which is in reference to the service master key.

```
USE HomeLending;
GO

SELECT
    b.name,
    a.crypt_type_desc
FROM
    sys.key_encryptions a
    INNER JOIN sys.symmetric_keys b
        ON a.key_id = b.symmetric_key_id
WHERE
    b.name = '##MS_DatabaseMasterKey##';
GO
```

Listing 5-4: Confirming protection of the database master key by the service master key.

The next step is to create a self-signed certificate that is protected by the database master key of our HomeLending database. All certificates created within SQL Server, as opposed to being imported, are self-signed. This associates the certificate to the database.

Certificates are created using the CREATE CERTIFICATE method. The arguments of this method include:

- **Certificate_Name**, the name of the certificate in the database and the means by which we will reference this certificate in our stored procedures.

- **WITH SUBJECT**, used to provide a descriptive reference to the certificate, for informational purposes.

Since this certificate will be used to protect the symmetric keys that encrypt and decrypt the data that has the sensitivity classification of "High", we will name this certificate MyHighCert, as shown in Listing 5-5.

```
USE HomeLending;
GO

CREATE CERTIFICATE MyHighCert
    WITH SUBJECT = 'Cert used for sensitive class of high';
GO
```

Listing 5-5: Creating the MyHighCert self-signed certificate.

An optional argument when creating a certificate is ENCRYPTION BY PASSWORD. This argument defines a password protection method of the certificate's private key. In our creation of the certificate we have chosen to not include this argument; by doing so we are specifying that the certificate is to be protected by the database master key.

The final key in our hierarchy is the symmetric key that will be used to encrypt the sensitive data. The choice of a symmetric key is based upon requirement 3, which is derived from our need for efficiency and strength. The symmetric key is created through the execution of the CREATE SYMMETRIC KEY method.

The arguments to this method include:

- **Key_name**, the unique name of the key, in the database, and the means by which we reference this key in our views and stored procedures.

- **WITH ALGORITHM**, which defines the algorithm used that directly affects the strength of the key.

- **ENCRYPTION BY**, which defines the protection method of the key. The key used in the ENCRYPTION BY argument can be a certificate, another symmetric key, asymmetric key or a password. We will use our MyHighCert certificate to achieve the seamless functionality that we are expecting.

Since this key will be used to protect data with the sensitivity classification of "High", we will name it HighSymKey1. Since requirement 3 requires a key length of 128 bits and the use of the AES algorithm, we use AES_128 for the WITH ALGORITHM argument, as shown in Listing 5-6.

```
USE HomeLending;
GO

-- A 128 bit Symmetric key (strong)
CREATE SYMMETRIC KEY HighSymKey1
    WITH ALGORITHM = AES_128
    ENCRYPTION BY CERTIFICATE MyHighCert;
GO
```

Listing 5-6: Creating the **HighSymKey1** symmetric key.

Granting Permission to Use the Symmetric Key

Once we have created our symmetric key we will need to define the database roles that have permissions to use it. This is accomplished through use of the GRANT method. In order to use this symmetric key, our database role will require VIEW DEFINITION permissions. Since the Sensitive_high database role is the only one that we are allowing to encrypt and decrypt data that has a sensitivity classification of "High", we will grant the VIEW DEFINITION permissions to that role.

```
USE HomeLending;
GO

-- Used By Sensitive_high
GRANT VIEW DEFINITION ON SYMMETRIC KEY::HighSymKey1
    TO Sensitive_high;
GO
```

Listing 5-7: Granting the **VIEW DEFINITION** permission to the **Sensitive_ high** database role.

Testing the Access to Key Hierarchy

Now that our encryption key hierarchy has been created, we need to verify that it is effective. The native functionality of the sys.symmetric_keys catalog view reveals the symmetric keys to which a user either has VIEW DEFINITION permissions directly granted, or has permission to access through membership of a database role that has been granted VIEW DEFINITION permissions.

Through the use of EXECUTE AS USER, we can impersonate another user within the database. The use of REVERT terminates the impersonation and returns us to our original user account. For our verification, we are selecting a user that is a member of the Sensitive_high database role, a user that is a member of the Sensitive_medium database role and a user that is a member of the Sensitive_low database role.

```
USE HomeLending;
GO

-- execute as a user who is a member of Sensitive_high role
EXECUTE AS USER = 'WOLFBA';
GO
SELECT * FROM sys.symmetric_keys;
GO
REVERT;
GO

-- execute as a user who is a member of Sensitive_medium
role
EXECUTE AS USER = 'KELLEYWB';
GO
SELECT * FROM sys.symmetric_keys;
GO
REVERT;
GO

-- execute as a user who is a member of Sensitive_low role
EXECUTE AS USER = 'JONESBF';
GO
SELECT * FROM sys.symmetric_keys;
GO
REVERT;
GO
```

Listing 5-8: Validating the access to key hierarchy.

Successful validation is confirmed by the fact that only the user that is a member of the `Sensitive_high` database role will return a row that reflects the metadata of our `HighSymKey1` symmetric key.

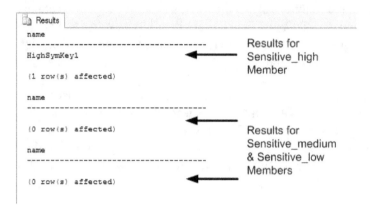

Figure 5-3: Results of key hierarchy access validation.

Required Schema Modifications

The `binary` data type stores the numeric representation of a value based upon a fixed length, which is set when the data type is used. For example, use of a binary data type with the fixed length of five would store the value of "0x4100000000" for the character of "A".

The `varbinary` data type stores the same numeric representation; but with a variable length. For example, the value of "A" is stored with the value of "0x41" while "ABC" is stored as "0x414243". The `binary` and `varbinary` data types both have a maximum length of 8,000 characters.

Cell-level encryption requires the encrypted value to be stored in a column that is the data type of `varbinary` since the encryption methods of `EncryptByAsymKey`, `EncryptByCert`, `EncryptByKey` and `EncryptByPassphrase` returns their cipher text in `varbinary`.

Creating the Encrypted Column

Earlier in this chapter, we discussed the levels of granularity that are available with cell-level encryption. In this exercise, we will be encrypting all cells within a single column with the same key.

In our review of our `Borrower_Identification` table, the column that contains the sensitivity classification of "High" is the `Identification_Value` column. Currently, this information is being stored in plain text using the `varchar` data type. In order to implement cell-level encryption, based on our previously-established key hierarchy, we will need to create a column in our table that will capture the encrypted value as a `varbinary` data type. Listing 5-9 shows how to accomplish this using the `ALTER TABLE` method.

```
USE HomeLending;
GO

ALTER TABLE dbo.Borrower_Identification ADD
    Identification_Value_E varbinary(MAX) NULL
GO
```

Listing 5-9: Adding a column to store `varbinary` data.

Since the column by the name of `Identification_Value` already exists, we chose to name this new column `Identification_Value_E`, with the "E" representing the fact that the column is encrypted. At a later point in this process we will drop the `Identification_Value` column, since we do not want to maintain storage of our sensitive data in plain text.

The `NULL` constraint to the column definition states that the column can accept the value of `NULL`. It is not our intention to allow `NULL` values in the column once cell-level encryption is in place; but since we will be adding this column to existing rows, we will temporarily permit the value of `NULL` to prevent an error when creating the column.

It is important to note that the `ALTER TABLE` method should be executed when the database is not in use by other users. The `ALTER TABLE` method implements a lock on the table during its processing. Large volumes of rows in a table that is being altered will result in a lengthy execution time and could result in lock contention, deadlocks and overall poor performance for other transactions that are attempting to access the table.

Populating the Encrypted Column

Now that we have added our new `Identification_Value_E` column, we need to populate the column with the encrypted values, based upon the plain text in the original `Identification_Value` column and the symmetric key `HighSymKey1`.

The script shown in Listing 5-10 opens the `HighSymKey1` symmetric key, allowing us to perform the encryption functions, and then updates the `Identification_Value_E` column in the `Borrower_Identification` table with the encrypted value, using the `EncryptByKey` method. An example of the syntax for this method is as follows:

```
EncryptByKey(Key_GUID([KeyName]),[Clear_Text],
             [Add_Authenticator],[Authenticator])
```

We are passing four arguments to the `EncryptByKey` method in order to perform the encryption:

- **Key_GUID**: A reference to the symmetric key that is used for encryption. The `Key_GUID` system function is used to return the GUID value of the key based upon its name. This GUID value is used by this method to locate the symmetric key.

- **Clear_Text**: The plain text value that we wish to encrypt. Since we are updating based upon the contents of the table, we supply the reference to the `Identification_Value` column.

- **Add_Authenticator**: A value indicating whether or not we want to use an **authenticator** with the encryption. The value of "1" indicates that it is to be used, while the value of "0", or the absence of this argument, indicates that it is not to be used.

- **Authenticator**: The value that is used for the authenticator.

An authenticator is a value that is hashed and appended to the plain text prior to encryption. This increases the strength of the resulting encrypted value since decryption requires the passing of the authenticator, if used. In the case of our sample database we will use the `Borrower_ID` column value as our authenticator, since it is a value that will not change for the row and identifies the borrower that the `Borrower_Identification` column references.

124

```
USE HomeLending;
GO

-- Opens the symmetric key for use
OPEN SYMMETRIC KEY HighSymKey1
    DECRYPTION BY CERTIFICATE MyHighCert;
GO

-- Performs the update of the record
UPDATE dbo.Borrower_Identification
    SET Identification_Value_E =
        EncryptByKey(
            Key_GUID('HighSymKey1'),
            Identification_Value,
            1,
            CONVERT(nvarchar(128),Borrower_ID)
        )
FROM
    dbo.Borrower_Identification;
GO

-- Closes the symmetric key
CLOSE SYMMETRIC KEY HighSymKey1;
GO
```

Listing 5-10: Encrypting the data for the `Identification_Value_E` column.

Note that if an authenticator is used and the value on which the authenticator is dependent changes, the result will be a failed decryption attempt.

Through the successful execution of the script in Listing 5-10, the plain text values that are stored in the `Identification_Value` column will have been encrypted and stored in the `Identification_Value_E` column. The next step in this process is to remove the plain text values, stored in the `Identification_Value` column, from the table. We can do this using the ALTER TABLE method and the DROP COLUMN argument, as shown in Listing 5-11.

```
USE HomeLending;
GO

ALTER TABLE dbo.Borrower_Identification
    DROP COLUMN Identification_Value;
GO
```

Listing 5-11: Dropping the plain text `Identification_Value` column.

125

One final step is to apply the extended property that reflects the sensitivity classification of the Identification_Value_E column, which is "High". This is accomplished through the execution of the sp_addextendedproperty system stored procedure, as demonstrated in Listing 5-12.

```
USE HomeLending;
GO

EXEC sp_addextendedproperty
    @name='Sensitivity_Class',
    @value='High',
    @level0type='SCHEMA',
    @level0name='dbo',
    @level1type='TABLE',
    @level1name='Borrower_Identification',
    @level2type='COLUMN',
    @level2name='Identification_Value_E';
GO
```

Listing 5-12: Documenting the encrypted column.

Views and Stored Procedures

The sensitive data that is contained within the Borrower_Identification table is now protected with cell-level encryption. Our next steps are to create the views and stored procedures via which our users can interact with the Borrower_Identification table. With the inclusion of cryptographic functionality to these objects we will need to pay careful attention to the handling of failed encryption and decryption efforts.

Failed Decryption Handling

Currently, when an attempt to open the symmetric key, and perform decryption, fails due to the user not having the appropriate permissions to the key, the value of NULL is returned. This is not very informative to the end user and does not differentiate a true NULL value from a failed decryption attempt. Therefore, we will present the following requirement:

126

Requirement 5: Handling unauthorized decryption attempts

When the value of NULL is returned by a failed decryption attempt, it will be replaced with the value "<SECURED VALUE>".

Data Modification Handling

Protecting the integrity of the encrypted data that is stored in the database is a critical concern. When a user updates or inserts a row that contains data in our high sensitivity column, the encryption key will need to be opened. If the user has the required permission to use the key, encryption will be applied and the transaction will be committed. However, if the user does not have the necessary permissions to the encryption key, the value that will be captured in the encrypted column will be a value of NULL, resulting in the loss of the value passed to the table.

By restricting insert or update activity to those who have permissions granted to the encryption key, we ensure that the value that is passed to the encrypted column contains valid encrypted data. Based on this observation, we define our final requirement:

Requirement 6: Restricting data modification

Transactions that update or insert rows into a table that contains encrypted columns are to be performed only by the members of roles who have been granted permissions to the corresponding keys. For better control of this requirement all data modifications will occur through stored procedures.

Creating the View

Requirement 2 denies all members of the Sensitive_high, Sensitive_medium and Sensitive_low permission to directly access the tables in our database. Access to the data within our tables is to be gained through views.

The script shown in Listing 5-13 creates a view called vwBorrower_Identification, which will reflect the columns that are contained within the base table.

The reference to the encrypted column, Identification_Value_E, will utilize the DecryptByKeyAutoCert method to decrypt the data. The DecryptByKeyAutoCert method performs, in a single command, the opening of any symmetric keys protected by the MyHighCert certificate, the decryption of the Identification_Value_E column, including the specified authenticator, and the closing of the symmetric keys protected by the MyHighCert certificate.

If a user who calls this view does not have the sufficient permissions granted to open the symmetric keys that are protected by the MyHighCert certificate, the decrypted value returned will be NULL. The script uses the COALESCE method to instead return a value of <SECURED VALUE>, if decryption fails. This fulfills the requirements of Requirement 5.

```
USE HomeLending;
GO

CREATE VIEW dbo.vwBorrower_Identification
AS

SELECT
    Borrower_Identification_ID,
    Borrower_ID,
    Identification_Type_ID,
    CONVERT(varchar(250),
        COALESCE(
            DecryptByKeyAutoCert (
                CERT_ID('MyHighCert'),
                NULL,
                Identification_Value_E,
                1,
                CONVERT(nvarchar(128), Borrower_ID)
            ),
            '<SECURED VALUE>'
        )
    ) AS Identification_Value
FROM
    dbo.Borrower_Identification;
GO
```

Listing 5-13: Creating the **vwBorrower_Identification** view.

Please note that we selected to return the column name as Identification_Value since it is a more intuitive name than the underlying Identification_Value_E column name.

128

The final step in implementing this view is to grant the appropriate permissions to it. In Requirement 6, we specified that all data modification activities would be managed through stored procedures; therefore we will only grant SELECT permissions to the view.

The Borrower_Information table contains four columns, three of which have the sensitivity classification of "Medium". Disclosure of the column that has the sensitivity classification of "High" is managed through the permissions to the symmetric key that decrypts it. There are no columns with the sensitivity classification of "Low"; therefore we will grant SELECT permissions only to the Sensitive_high and Sensitive_medium database roles.

```
USE HomeLending;
GO


GRANT SELECT ON dbo.vwBorrower_Identification
    TO Sensitive_high, Sensitive_medium;
GO
```

Listing 5-14: Granting permission to access the view.

Let's now verify that the permissions are effective and that the decryption performs as expected. As described earlier, we'll use EXECUTE AS USER to impersonate a user that is a member of the Sensitive_high database role, a user that is a member of the Sensitive_medium database role and a user that is a member of the Sensitive_low database role, as shown in Listing 5-15.

```
USE HomeLending;
GO


-- execute as a user who is a member of Sensitive_high role
EXECUTE AS USER = 'WOLFBA';
GO
SELECT * FROM dbo.vwBorrower_Identification;
GO
REVERT;
GO


-- execute as a user who is a member of Sensitive_medium
role
EXECUTE AS USER = 'KELLEYWB';
GO
SELECT * FROM dbo.vwBorrower_Identification;
GO
REVERT;
```

```
GO

-- execute as a user who is a member of Sensitive_low role
EXECUTE AS USER = 'JONESBF';
GO
SELECT * FROM dbo.vwBorrower_Identification;
GO
REVERT;
GO
```

Listing 5-15: Verification of permissions to vwBorrower_Identification.

The result of this verification will reflect that rows were returned for the queries from the Sensitive_high and Sensitive_medium members; but since permissions did not exist for the Sensitive_low member the actual rows will not be returned. Instead the following will appear:

```
(180593 row(s) affected)
(180593 row(s) affected)
Msg 229, Level 14, State 5, Line 1
The SELECT permission was denied on the object
'vwBorrower_Identification', database 'HomeLending',
schema 'dbo'.
```

The permissions set for this view are not to be confused with the permissions set to the keys that are used to encrypt and decrypt. These permissions are reflected through the actual results that come from the execution of this view. For example, the WOLFBA user will have the decrypted version of the encrypted data appearing in their results; while the KELLEYWB user will see the value "<SECURED VALUE>" in the sensitive column.

Creating the Stored Procedures

Requirement 1 dictates that only members of the Sensitive_high database role can execute INSERT and UPDATE methods on a table that contains columns with the sensitivity classification of "High". We have already established that the Borrower_Identification table contains one of these columns.

In addition, Requirement 2 dictates that all interaction with tables is to be performed through views and stored procedures. Requirement 6 dictates that all data modifications occur through stored procedures. In compliance with these requirements we will create two stored procedures.

The first stored procedure, named `Update_Borrower_Identification`, will perform the following:

- Open the `HighSymKey1` symmetric key with the `MyHighCert` certificate through the `OPEN SYMMETRIC KEY` method.

- Execute the `UPDATE` method while using the `EncryptByKey` method to encrypt the value that is passed in the `@Identification_Value` argument. This encryption includes the use of the `@Borrower_ID` argument as the authenticator.

- Catch the occurrence of an error so that the stored procedure fails gracefully. This is accomplished by the use of the `TRY...CATCH` method.

- Check the `HighSymKey1` symmetric key to determine if it is open before attempting to close it through the `sys.openkeys` catalog view. If it is open, the key is closed using the `CLOSE SYMMETRIC KEY` method.

Listing 5-16 shows the full code for the stored procedure.

```
USE HomeLending;
GO

CREATE PROCEDURE dbo.Update_Borrower_Identification
    @Borrower_Identification_ID bigint,
    @Borrower_ID bigint,
    @Identification_Value varchar(250)
AS
BEGIN TRY

    -- Opens the symmetric key for use
    OPEN SYMMETRIC KEY HighSymKey1
        DECRYPTION BY CERTIFICATE MyHighCert;

    -- Performs the update of the record
    UPDATE dbo.Borrower_Identification
        SET Identification_Value_E =
            EncryptByKey(
                Key_GUID('HighSymKey1'),
                @Identification_Value,
                1,
                CONVERT(nvarchar(128),@Borrower_ID)
            )
    WHERE
```

```
            Borrower_Identification_ID =
                @Borrower_Identification_ID;

END TRY
BEGIN CATCH
    -- Returns the error information
    SELECT
        ERROR_NUMBER() AS ErrorNumber,
        ERROR_SEVERITY() AS ErrorSeverity,
        ERROR_STATE() AS ErrorState,
        ERROR_MESSAGE() AS ErrorMessage;
END CATCH

-- Closes the symmetric key if open
IF(EXISTS(
            SELECT
                *
            FROM
                sys.openkeys
            WHERE
                key_guid = Key_GUID('HighSymKey1')
        )
    )
    BEGIN
        CLOSE SYMMETRIC KEY HighSymKey1;
    END
GO
```

Listing 5-16: The stored procedure through which authorized users can update sensitive data.

The second stored procedure, named `Insert_Borrower_Identification`, will perform the following:

- Open the `HighSymKey1` symmetric key with the `MyHighCert` certificate through the `OPEN SYMMETRIC KEY` method.

- Execute the `INSERT` method while using the `EncryptByKey` method to encrypt the value that is passed in the `@Identification_Value` argument. This encryption includes the use of the `@Borrower_ID` argument as the authenticator.

- Capture the new `Borrower_Identification_ID` of the inserted record, which is referenced through the use of `@@IDENTITY`, and returns it as the result of the stored procedure.

132

- Catch the occurrence of an error so that the stored procedure fails gracefully. This is accomplished by the use of the TRY...CATCH method.

- Check the HighSymKey1 symmetric key to determine if it is open before attempting to close it through the sys.openkeys catalog view. If it is open, the key is closed using the CLOSE SYMMETRIC KEY method.

Listing 5-17 shows the full code for the stored procedure.

```
USE HomeLending;
GO

CREATE PROCEDURE dbo.Insert_Borrower_Identification
    @Borrower_ID bigint,
    @Identification_Type_ID int,
    @Identification_Value varchar(250)
AS
BEGIN TRY

    -- Opens the symmetric key for use
    OPEN SYMMETRIC KEY HighSymKey1
        DECRYPTION BY CERTIFICATE MyHighCert;

    -- Performs the update of the record
    INSERT INTO dbo.Borrower_Identification
        (
            Borrower_ID,
            Identification_Type_ID,
            Identification_Value_E
        )
        VALUES
        (
            @Borrower_ID,
            @Identification_Type_ID,
            EncryptByKey(
                Key_GUID('HighSymKey1'),
                @Identification_Value,
                1,
                CONVERT(nvarchar(128),@Borrower_ID)
            )
        );

    -- Captures the new Borrower_Identification_ID value
    SELECT @@IDENTITY;

END TRY
```

```
BEGIN CATCH
    -- Returns the error information
    SELECT
        ERROR_NUMBER() AS ErrorNumber,
        ERROR_SEVERITY() AS ErrorSeverity,
        ERROR_STATE() AS ErrorState,
        ERROR_MESSAGE() AS ErrorMessage;
END CATCH

-- Closes the symmetric key if open
IF(EXISTS(
            SELECT
                *
            FROM
                sys.openkeys
            WHERE
                key_guid = Key_GUID('HighSymKey1')
        )
    )
    BEGIN
        CLOSE SYMMETRIC KEY HighSymKey1;
    END
GO
```

Listing 5-17: The stored procured through which authorized users can insert sensitive data.

The final step in implementing these stored procedures is to grant the appropriate permissions to them. Requirement 6 allows the INSERT or UPDATE methods to be executed, if an encrypted column exists; only when the database role that performs the INSERT or UPDATE method has permissions granted to the key that performs the encryption.

The encrypted column in the Borrower_Information table, Information_Value_E, is encrypted by the HighSymKey1 symmetric key to which only the Sensitive_high database role has permissions to utilize; therefore, we will grant EXECUTE permissions to our two stored procedures only to the members of the Sensitive_high database role, as shown in Listing 5-18.

```
USE HomeLending;
GO

-- Grant Execute Permissions to Sensitive_high database
role
GRANT EXECUTE ON dbo.Update_Borrower_Identification
```

```
    TO Sensitive_high;
GO

-- Grant Execute Permissions to Sensitive_high database
role
GRANT EXECUTE ON dbo.Insert_Borrower_Identification
    TO Sensitive_high;
GO
```

Listing 5-18: Granting, to the `sensitive_high` role, permission to execute the two stored procedures.

Summary

Through this demonstration we have successfully implemented cell-level encryption for the `Borrower_Identification` table of our `HomeLending` database. We have encrypted one column of one table among many more, throughout our database, that beg for similar attention.

- The application of cell-level encryption employs all of the concepts that have been presented in the previous chapters.

- Through the understanding of sensitive data we executed the data classification process.

- The extended properties that were created through the data classification process were utilized to identify the columns that must have the cell-level encryption applied.

- Through the implementation of our database roles that define the privileges to sensitive data, we were able to precisely control access to data and cryptography functionality.

- The schema design that we implemented that segregated our sensitive data from data of lesser sensitivity allowed us to create views and stored procedures that manage functionality at a very granular level.

- Through our understanding of the key hierarchy and complexities of encryption key algorithms, we were able to implement a very manageable, seamless and efficient solution for executing cryptographic functions.

Now let's explore how encryption can provide protection to the entire database with the Transparent Data Encryption (TDE) feature of SQL Server 2008.

CHAPTER 6: TRANSPARENT DATA ENCRYPTION

Keyless entry for automobiles was first introduced by American Motors Corporation in 1983 and, today, there are a variety of methods that are available that permit the user to gain access to their automobile without inserting a physical key into the door lock. These include pushing a button on a device that transmits a radio frequency, entering a code into a key pad located beneath the driver's side door handle, or possessing a device, called a fob, that is detected by the automobile's security system.

Of these devices, only the fob offers *transparency* to the owner of the vehicle. The fob is recognized by the security system and the door is automatically unlocked; in other words, the fob holder is granted access to the vehicle without any distinguishable action required on his or her part. If a person who does not possess the fob attempts to open the door of the automobile, the door remains locked, denying access into the vehicle.

The experience of the car owner in possession of a fob is similar to the experience of the user attempting to gain access to a database in which **Transparent Data Encryption (TDE)** has been enabled. TDE is distinct from other techniques discussed in this book in that it secures data by encrypting the physical files of the database, rather than the data itself. The data files for a given database are encrypted using a **database encryption key** in the user database. This key references a key hierarchy in the Master database, and this dependency prevents the data files from being viewed outside their instance.

Therefore, a valid user can access the decrypted contents of the database files without any distinguishable actions, and without even being aware that the underlying data files are encrypted. However, a would-be data thief, who has obtained access to the data files through a stolen backup file, will find he or she is unable to access the data it contains. Overall, this is a straightforward, low-impact feature that has great security benefits; the only caveat being that it requires SQL Server 2008 Enterprise Edition.

In this chapter we will explore the considerations of TDE that must be understood prior to its use. We will also walk through an example of implementing and validating TDE using the HomeLending database. Finally, we will cover the process of removing TDE, should the need arise.

How TDE Works

Transparent Data Encryption (TDE) was introduced in SQL Server 2008, as a feature of the *Enterprise Edition* of that product. The *Developer Edition* of SQL Server 2008 also offers TDE, but its license limits its use to development and testing only.

As noted above, TDE's specific purpose is to protect data at rest by encrypting the physical files of the database, rather than the data. These physical files include the database file (.mdf), the transaction log file (.ldf) and the backup files (.bak).

The protection of the database files is accomplished through an encryption key hierarchy that exists externally from the database in which TDE has been enabled. The exception to this is the **database encryption key**, which was introduced to the database encryption key hierarchy (see Chapter 4) specifically to support the TDE feature, and is used to perform the encryption of the database files.

In Figure 6-1, the key hierarchy, and their required location of each key, is illustrated. The service master key exists at the instance level. The database master key and certificate at the Master database are used to protect the database encryption key that is located at the user database, which is the HomeLending database in our example. The database encryption key is then used to decrypt the database files of the user database.

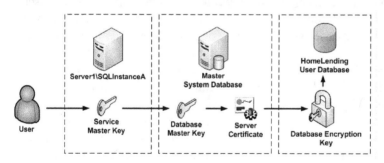

Figure 6-1: TDE Encryption Key Hierarchy.

The dependency upon the encryption key hierarchy in the Master database, as well as the instance, prevents the database files from being restored to an instance of SQL Server that does not contain the referenced keys. This level of protection is a great comfort if a backup tape that contains your database backup files were to fall into the wrong hands.

Additionally, the encryption of the backup files prevents the plain text values that are contained within the database being disclosed by opening the backup files using a text editor and scanning its contents. The details regarding this scenario will be covered later in this chapter.

Benefits and Disadvantages of TDE

Comparing TDE to cell-level encryption is a bit like comparing apples to oranges. They are solutions for different challenges. TDE offers general protection to the database while cell-level encryption offers specific protection to data. I would encourage you to consider using TDE in conjunction with other encryption and obfuscation methods, for a layered approach to protection. To determine whether or not TDE should be part of your protection strategy for sensitive data, consider the following benefits and disadvantages.

Benefits

- Implementation of TDE does not require any schema modifications.

- Since the physical data files and not the data itself are encrypted, the primary keys and indexes on the data are unaffected, and so optimal query execution can be maintained.

- The performance impact on the database is minimal. In their white paper titled "*Database Encryption in SQL Server 2008 Enterprise Edition*", Microsoft estimates the performance degradation for TDE to be 3–5%, while cell-level encryption is estimated to be 20–28%. Of course, the impact well may vary, depending upon your specific environment, and volume of data.

- The decryption process is invisible to the end user.

Disadvantages

- Use of TDE renders negligible any benefits to be gained from backup compression, as the backup files will be only minimally compressed. It is not recommended to use these two features together on the same database.

139

- TDE does not provide the same granular control, specific to a user or database role, as is offered by cell-level encryption.

- TDE is available only with SQL Server 2008, *Enterprise Edition* and so will probably not be available to all installations within your environment.

Considerations when Implementing TDE

Prior to implementing TDE, there are several issues to take into consideration, discussed over the following sections.

Master Key Interdependency

The process of implementing TDE involves the creation of a database master key and certificate, or asymmetric key, on the Master database. Only one database master key can be created for a given database so any other user databases that share the instance, and have TDE implemented, will share a dependency upon the Master database master key.

This interdependency increases the importance of performing a backup of the Master database master key to ensure the continued accessibility of the TDE-enabled databases.

Performance Impact on TempDB

When TDE is initially implemented, the physical file of the TempDB system database is also encrypted. Since the TempDB database contains temporary data from the TDE-enabled database, its encryption is required to maintain full protection by this feature; otherwise the information that is temporarily stored in the TempDB database from the TDE enabled databases would be exposed through the physical files of TempDB.

The TempDB database is used by all user and system databases in the instance to store temporary objects, such as temporary tables, cursors and work tables for spooling. It also provides row versioning and the ability to rollback transactions.

Once the `TempDB` database is encrypted, any reference and use of this database by other databases, regardless of whether they have TDE enabled or not, will require encryption and decryption. While this encryption and decryption of the `TempDB` database files remains transparent to the user, it does have a minimal performance impact on the entire instance. Microsoft has estimated the entire impact of TDE on a SQL Server instance to be 3–5% depending on the server environment and data volume.

TDE and Decryption

TDE is designed to protect data *at rest* by encrypting the physical data files rather than the data itself. This level of protection prevents the data and backup files from being opened in a text editor to expose the file's contents.

TDE encryption occurs prior to writing data to disk, and the data is decrypted when it is queried and recalled into memory. This encryption and decryption occurs without any additional coding or data type modifications; thus it's transparency. Once the data is recalled from disk, into memory, it is no longer considered to be at rest. It has become data *in transit*, which is beyond the scope of this feature. As such, alongside TDE, you should consider applying additional supporting layers of protection to your sensitive data, to ensure complete protection from unauthorized disclosure. For example, you may wish to implement, in addition to TDE, encrypted database connections, cell-level encryption, or one-way encryption. For additional data in transit protection that is required, externally from the database, you may need to consult with, or defer to, your Network Administration team.

Backup and Recovery

As noted previously, TDE prevents the backup files from being opened by a plain text editor. It also limits the recovery of the database backup file to the instance that holds the encryption key hierarchy that was in existence at the time the backup was created.

As illustrated in Figure 6-1, backup files of databases with TDE enabled are encrypted using a key hierarchy that includes the service master key of the SQL Server instance, the database master key and certificate for the `Master` database.

Despite this dependency, none of these keys are included with the standard database backup, and must be backed up separately via the following commands (see Listing 4-8, in Chapter 4, for example usage):

- **BACKUP SERVICE MASTER KEY** to backup of the service master key.

- **BACKUP MASTER KEY** to backup of a database master key.

- **BACKUP CERTIFICATE** to backup the certificate.

This behavior is one of the security benefits of TDE. In order to restore the encrypted data to another instance of SQL Server, a user needs to recover the service master key backup file, the `Master` database master key backup file and the `Master` database certificate private key, prior to recovering the database backup file.

The database encryption key that is created in the user database, in which TDE has been implemented, is included in the standard database backup. It is stored in the boot record of the database file so that it can be accessed and used to decrypt the user database.

When the service master key and database master key are backed up, it is recommended to store their backup files in a separate location from the database files. This separation will ensure continued protection of the encrypted data in the event that the database backup media is stolen or compromised.

TDE and Replication

If the TDE-enabled database is part of a replication setup, the subscribing database must also have TDE implemented. The data that is traveling between the databases will be in plain text and is vulnerable to unauthorized disclosure. A method of encrypting connections, such as secure socket layers (SSL) or Internet protocol security (IPSec), is recommended.

TDE and FileStream Data

The `FILESTREAM` data type stores large unstructured objects, such as documents and images, in an integrated physical file that is separate from the database file. When TDE is implemented on a user database that contains `FILESTREAM` data, the filestream files remain unencrypted.

Implementing TDE

In this section, we will implement TDE using the `HomeLending` database. Our TDE implementation, in comparison to cell-level encryption, will be very simple. There are no modifications to the schema required, there are no permissions that need to be granted to database users and roles in order to use TDE, and there are no additional database objects that must be created to perform the encryption and decryption methods.

On the other hand, the person performing the implementation of TDE does require specific permissions; namely `CONTROL` permissions on the `Master` and `HomeLending` databases. It is recommended to perform this process while the database is not in use by other users.

Backup before Proceeding

It is a general best practice to backup a database prior to making modifications. However, it is especially important when implementing TDE, in order to ensure that, should the TDE implementation need to be reversed, you can cleanly recover the database in its original form.

In addition, by performing a database backup, a new checkpoint will be established in the transaction log. The creation of a checkpoint truncates all inactive items in your transaction log prior to the new checkpoint. This will ensure that your transaction log is free from unencrypted items, prior to the TDE implementation. Listing 6-1 shows the backup command for the `HomeLending` database.

```
USE HomeLending;
GO

BACKUP DATABASE HomeLending
    TO DISK = 'D:\HomeLending\Backup\HomeLending.bak'
    WITH NOFORMAT,
    INIT,
    NAME = 'HomeLending-Full Database Backup',
    SKIP,
    NOREWIND,
    NOUNLOAD,
    STATS = 10
GO
```

Listing 6-1: Backing up the HomeLending database, prior to TDE.

With the backup successfully completed, we can begin the process of implementing TDE.

The Master Database

Our first step is to create a database master key for our Master database, using the CREATE MASTER KEY method, as shown in Listing 6-2.

```
USE master;
GO

CREATE MASTER KEY
    ENCRYPTION BY PASSWORD = 'MyStr0ngP@ssw0rd2009';
GO
```

Listing 6-2: Creating the database master key in the Master database.

Notice that, while ENCRYPTED BY PASSWORD is a required argument to the method, our intent, as in Chapter 5, is to instead protect the database master key with the service master key. This option is automatically available to us, upon creation of the database master key.

A search against the sys.key_encryptions catalog view for the ##MS_ DatabaseMasterKey## key, as shown in Listing 6-3, returns ENCRYPTION BY MASTER KEY, in reference to the service master key.

```
USE master;
GO
```

144

```
SELECT
    b.name,
    a.crypt_type_desc
FROM
    sys.key_encryptions a
    INNER JOIN sys.symmetric_keys b
        ON a.key_id = b.symmetric_key_id
WHERE
    b.name = '##MS_DatabaseMasterKey##';
GO
```

Listing 6-3: Confirming protection of the database master key by the service master key.

The next step is to create a self-signed certificate that is protected by the database master key of our Master database. All certificates created within SQL Server, as opposed to being imported, are self-signed. This associates the certificate to the database.

Certificates are created using the CREATE CERTIFICATE method, as described in the previous chapter in Listing 5-5. Since this certificate is located in the Master database and will be used to protect the database encryption key of our HomeLending database, we will name this certificate MasterCert, as shown in Listing 6-4.

```
USE master;
GO

CREATE CERTIFICATE MasterCert
    WITH SUBJECT = 'Cert used for TDE';
GO
```

Listing 6-4: Creating the MasterCert self-signed .

As for Listing 5-5, by omitting the ENCRYPTION BY PASSWORD argument, we are specifying that the certificate is to be protected by the database master key.

At this point in the process you should perform a backup of the certificate with its private key, using the BACKUP CERTIFICATE command shown in Listing 6-5. In the event that the HomeLending database needs to be restored, this certificate and its private key will be required.

```
USE master;
GO

BACKUP CERTIFICATE MasterCert
  TO FILE = 'D:\HomeLending\Backup\MasterCert.bak'
```

```
      WITH PRIVATE KEY (
            FILE = 'D:\HomeLending\Backup\MasterCert.pvk',
                ENCRYPTION BY PASSWORD = 'MyB@ckUpP@ssw0rd');
GO
```

Listing 6-5: Backing up the `MasterCert` certificate.

Since our `MasterCert` certificate is protected by the `Master` database master key, the `DECRYPTION BY PASSWORD` argument is not included in the `WITH PRIVATE KEY` argument of this command.

The User Database

Having created the database master key and the `MasterCert` certificate in the `Master` database, we are ready to create the database encryption key for the `HomeLending` database which we will use to perform the cryptographic functions for the physical files of our database.

The database encryption key is created using the `CREATE DATABASE ENCRYPTION KEY` command. The arguments to this method include:

- **WITH ALGORITHM**: Specifies the algorithm used, which in turn dictates the strength of the key.

- **ENCRYPTION BY**: Defines the protection method of the key. The key used in the `ENCRYPTION BY` argument can be a certificate or an asymmetric key that is located in the `Master` database.

Listing 6-6 shows the exact command used for the `HomeLending` database's database encryption key.

```
USE HomeLending;
GO

CREATE DATABASE ENCRYPTION KEY
    WITH ALGORITHM = AES_128
    ENCRYPTION BY SERVER CERTIFICATE MasterCert;
GO
```

Listing 6-6: Creating the `HomeLending` database encryption key.

The `AES_128` option specifies Advanced Encryption Standard (AES) with a 128 bit key length, and we protect the database encryption key with the `MasterCert` certificate that was created in the `Master` database.

The final step in the setup process of TDE is to enable it. This is accomplished by executing the ALTER DATABASE command with the SET ENCRYPTION ON argument.

```
USE HomeLending;
GO

ALTER DATABASE HomeLending
    SET ENCRYPTION ON;
GO
```

Listing 6-7: Enabling TDE.

At this point, an **encryption scan** occurs, which is the process by which the physical files of the database are scanned and encrypted. Included in this scan process are the database files, TempDB database files and transaction log files.

Transaction log files contain information that is used to maintain data integrity and are used in the restoration process. Within these files are a series of smaller units called **virtual log files** (VLFs). These VLFs contain records that pertain to transactions within the database file. Prior to the implementation of TDE, these VLFs contain unencrypted data. During the encryption scan any pages that have been in the buffer cache and modified, known as **dirty pages**, are written to disk, a new VLF is created and the prior inactive VLFs are truncated. This results in a transaction log that only contains encrypted data.

The duration of the encryption scan will vary depending upon the size of the database files. Once the process has completed, the encryption_state column in the sys.dm_database_encryption_keys dynamic management view will reflect the encryption state of "encrypted," and will show the value of "3" in this column, for our HomeLending database.

Verifying TDE

Once the implementation of TDE is complete there are a few ways you can verify that these steps indeed succeeded.

Using Dm_Database_Encryption_Keys

Dynamic management views (DMV) are built-in views that provide metadata regarding the settings, health and properties of SQL Server instances and databases. The `sys.dm_database_encryption_keys` DMV presents information about the database encryption keys used in a given database, as well as the encryption state of the database.

> **NOTE:**
>
> Database encryption keys are only utilized for the benefit of the TDE feature of SQL Server 2008; therefore this DMV is not available in SQL Server 2005.

Through the use of a query in which the `sys.dm_database_encryption_keys` DMV and the `sys.databases` catalog view are joined through the `database_id` column, we are able to determine the success of the TDE implementation, as demonstrated in Listing 6-8.

```
USE master;
GO

SELECT
    db.name,
    db.is_encrypted,
    dm.encryption_state,
    dm.percent_complete,
    dm.key_algorithm,
    dm.key_length
FROM
    sys.databases db
    LEFT OUTER JOIN sys.dm_database_encryption_keys dm
        ON db.database_id = dm.database_id;
GO
```

Listing 6-8: Verifying TDE using `dm_database_encryption_keys`.

A return value of "1" for the `is_encrypted` column of the `sys.databases` catalog view indicates that the database has been encrypted through TDE.

The value of the `encryption_state` column from the `sys.dm_database_encryption_keys` DMV reflects whether or not the encryption process is complete. A value of "3" indicates that the encryption process is complete. A value of "2" in this column indicates that the encryption process is in progress. The percent_complete column from the same DMV indicates the progress of the encryption process. This column only reflects a value other than "0" when the database encryption state is in the process of changing (being encrypted or decrypted).

In this sample query, I added the key_algorithm and key_length columns to illustrate an interesting dynamic in regard to the TempDB database, as shown in the results in Table 6-1.

name	is_ encrypted	encryption_ state	percent_ complete	key_ algorithm	key_ length
tempdb	0	3	0	AES	256
HomeLending	1	3	0	AES	128
model	0	NULL	NULL	NULL	NULL
master	0	NULL	NULL	NULL	NULL
msdb	0	NULL	NULL	NULL	NULL

Table 6-1: Results of TDE verification query.

As previously noted, the encryption of the TempDB is a byproduct of implementing TDE on any given database within an instance of SQL Server. The is_encrypted column for our HomeLending database contains the value of "1" which indicates that it has been successfully encrypted; but the TempDB contains the value of "0", while the values in the other columns indicate that encryption has taken place. This is because the TempDB database is encrypted outside of the established TDE key hierarchy.

This is further emphasized by the algorithm that is used to encrypt the TempDB database. As you will recall, the creation of the database encryption key for the HomeLending database was designated as AES_128, which uses a key length of 128 bits. The results of this query show that the TempDB database is actually using a key length of 256 bits.

The reason for the separate encryption process lies in the inherent behavior of the TempDB database; when the SQL Server instance is stopped and started the TempDB database is dropped and recreated. This can be verified by performing the following steps:

- **Stop** the SQL Server instance.
- **Start** the SQL Server instance.

- **Execute** SELECT * FROM SYS.DATABASES, using the Master database.

The result of the third step will reveal that the column titled CREATE_DATE for the TempDB database will be approximately the date and time that you restarted the SQL Server instance. When the sys.dm_database_encryption_keys DMV is executed, the database encryption key for the TempDB database will still be included in the results and the column titled CREATE_DATE will also reflect the time that the instance was restarted. This illustrates that when the TempDB database is recreated so is its database encryption key.

At first glance the comparison of the CREATE_DATE columns of the sys.databases and sys.dm_database_encryption_keys DMV may raise concern since they do not match; but consider that the sys.dm_database_encryption_keys DMV reflects the date and time in Greenwich Mean Time (GMT) while the sys.databases catalog view reflects the date and time according to your time zone. Depending on your location this may appear to be in the future or in the past. In my case, being on Eastern Standard Time (EST) in the United States the sys.dm_database_encryption_keys DMV CREATE_DATE is five hours into the future.

Verification through Backup and Recovery

Another method of verifying the success of a TDE implementation is to perform a backup of the database, after TDE has been enabled, as shown in Listing 6-9. When doing so, make sure not to overwrite the backup file that was created prior to implementing TDE.

```
USE HomeLending;
GO

BACKUP DATABASE HomeLending
  TO DISK = 'D:\HomeLending\Backup\HomeLending_PostTDE.bak'
  WITH NOFORMAT,
  INIT,
  NAME = 'HomeLending-Full Database Backup',
  SKIP,
  NOREWIND,
  NOUNLOAD,
  STATS = 10
GO
```

Listing 6-9: Backing up the HomeLending database after TDE is implemented.

The next step is to compare the contents of the pre-TDE and post-TDE backup files, by opening both files up in a simple text editor such as Notepad, Wordpad or Textpad. We can perform a search within the pre-TDE backup file for the plain text of a known sensitive data value. For example, we will search for the value of "*319726 Rocky Fabien Avenue*" which is contained in the Borrower_Address table in the HomeLending database.

This search reveals the searched value in plain text, as shown in Figure 6-2. In addition, if you were to manually scan through the backup file, you would find that the metadata of our database objects, such as tables, views, stored procedures and user defined functions are revealed in plain text.

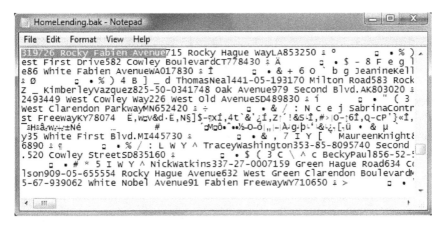

Figure 6-2: Backup File – Unencrypted.

The same search on our post-TDE backup file will result in the message box shown in Figure 6-3, stating that it cannot find the requested value. This is because the entire backup file, including the metadata of our database objects, has been encrypted and no longer contains any plain text values.

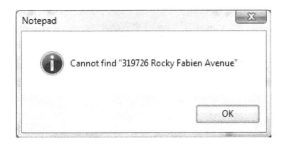

Figure 6-3: Search Results in Encrypted Backup File.

One final test in regard to the backup file is to attempt to restore the post-TDE backup file onto a different instance than the one in which the HomeLending database resides, using the RESTORE DATABASE command, as shown in Listing 6-10.

```
USE master;
GO

RESTORE DATABASE HomeLending
    FROM DISK = 'D:\HomeLending\Backup\HomeLending_PostTDE.
bak'
    WITH FILE = 1,
    NOUNLOAD,
    REPLACE,
    STATS = 10
GO
```

Listing 6-10: Attempting to restore the HomeLending database.

This attempt will return an error message that states that the certificate at the Master database level, in which the HomeLending database encryption key is protected, does not exist; therefore the attempt will fail.

```
Msg 33111, Level 16, State 3, Line 2
Cannot find server certifiate with thumbprint...


Msg 3013, Level 16, State 3, Line 2
RESTORE DATABASE is terminating abnormally
```

Using EXECUTE AS

Finally, we can perform a test to determine that the data that is contained within the encrypted HomeLending database files can be read by valid users of the database, as shown in Listing 6-11. As described previously in Chapter 5, we use EXECUTE AS USER to impersonate various users within the database and test their ability to access the encrypted data. The use of REVERT terminates the impersonation and returns us to our original user account.

```
USE HomeLending;
GO

-- execute as a user who is a member of Sensitive_high role
EXECUTE AS USER = 'WOLFBA';
```

```
GO
SELECT * FROM dbo.Borrower;
GO
REVERT;
GO

-- execute as a user who is a member of Sensitive_medium
role
EXECUTE AS USER = 'KELLEYWB';
GO
SELECT * FROM dbo.Borrower;
GO
REVERT;
GO

-- execute as a user who is a member of Sensitive_low role
EXECUTE AS USER = 'JONESBF';
GO
SELECT * FROM dbo.Borrower;
GO
REVERT;
GO
```

Listing 6-11: Verifying TDE using EXECUTE AS queries.

Each query in the above script successfully returns the contents of the Borrower table within the HomeLending database. This demonstrates that the automatic decryption is functioning as expected, and verifies that permissions to the appropriate database objects are not affected.

Please note that if the exercises for implementing cell-level encryption, presented in Chapter 5, have been completed within the same database that is being used in the TDE exercises, the query in Listing 6-11 will fail since permissions to all tables were denied to the Sensitive_high, Sensitive_medium and Sensitive_low database roles. This can be overcome by granting SELECT permissions to these database roles to the Borrower table.

Reversing the Implementation of TDE

It was once said that the only things certain in life are death and taxes. It could be argued that change is another certainty. You may find yourself in a situation where TDE has been implemented, you have validated that it works, are ready for users to begin using the newly-encrypted database and then, lo-and-behold, a request to reverse TDE comes your way.

> **Boss:** "I would like you to proceed with implementing TDE immediately ..."

> **DBA:** "Cool, I'll get right on it."
> *(DBA Implements TDE)*

> **Boss:** "Hey, as I was saying yesterday: I would like you to proceed with implementing TDE next week after our presentation to the Technology Committee."

> **DBA:** "No problem ... ah ..."
> *(Begin reversal process)*

If, at the time this request comes your way, no transactions have been performed on the encrypted database then you can reverse the TDE implementation using the following steps:

1. **Restore the backup file** of the `HomeLending` database that was created before TDE was implemented.

2. **Drop the certificate** that was created in the `Master` database. This should only be done if there are no other user databases in the instance that have been TDE-enabled. If there are other user databases in the instance that have TDE enabled, you will want to leave the `Master` database items untouched.

3. **Drop the database master key** that was created in the `Master` database. This should only be done if there are no other user databases in the instance that have TDE enabled. Otherwise, you will want to leave the `Master` database items untouched.

4. **Restart the instance** in which the `HomeLending` database resides. If there are not any other user databases on the instance that have TDE implemented, this action will force the recreation of the `TempDB` database in an unencrypted format.

Listing 6-12 shows the code to implement these steps.

```
USE master;
GO

RESTORE DATABASE HomeLending
    FROM DISK = 'D:\HomeLending\Backup\HomeLending.bak'
    WITH FILE = 1,
    NOUNLOAD,
    REPLACE,
    STATS = 10;
GO

DROP CERTIFICATE MasterCert;
GO

DROP MASTER KEY;
GO

-- Restart Instance Though SQL Server Management Studio:
-- Right-Click instance and click on "Restart" option.
```

Listing 6-12: Reversing TDE when no transactions have occurred.

If the request to reverse the implementation of TDE comes after transactions have occurred, or a copy of the pre-TDE backup file is no longer available, the following steps can be performed:

1. **Alter the `HomeLending` database** to have the ENCRYPTION option set to the value of OFF.

2. **Wait until the decryption process is complete**. Use the `sys.dm_database_encryption_keys` DMV to determine its status. A value of "1" returned in the `encryption_status` column indicates that the decryption is complete.

3. **Drop the database encryption key** for the `HomeLending` database.

4. **Restart the instance** in which the `HomeLending` database resides. If there are not any other user databases on the instance that have TDE implemented, this action will force the recreation of the `TempDB` database in an unencrypted format.

Listing 6-13 shows the code to implement these steps.

```
USE HomeLending;
GO

ALTER DATABASE HomeLending
    SET ENCRYPTION OFF;
GO

-- Before proceeding, wait until the decryption process is
complete.
-- Use the sys.dm_database_encryption_keys dmv to determine
this.

DROP DATABASE ENCRYPTION KEY;
GO

-- Restart Instance Though SQL Server Management Studio:
-- Right-Click instance and click on "Restart" option.
```

Listing 6-13: Reversing TDE after transactions have occurred.

We will need to keep the certificate and database master key that was setup in the `Master` database, since there will remain some dependencies upon these keys that affect the recoverability of the database.

It is recommended to perform either of these removal options while the database is not in use by other users. In addition, it is always recommended that a backup be made of the database, the database master key and certificate prior to reversing TDE.

Summary

Through this demonstration we have successfully implemented TDE for the `HomeLending` database and validated that it is enabled. In addition, the steps to reverse TDE have been provided in the event that it is requested.

While TDE does not offer the granularity of protection that cell-level encryption offers, it does provide a level of protection that cannot be achieved through cell-level encryption. This feature provides a means to render unreadable the plain text that would otherwise be disclosed in the database backup files.

Thanks to the encryption key hierarchy that is external to the database, additional protection is offered by restricting restoration of the encrypted database to the instance from which the backup files were created.

Implementing TDE in conjunction with cell-level encryption provides a layered approach to data security, which enhances its effectiveness. Another option for protecting sensitive data that is available is one-way encryption, also referred to as hashing. One-way encryption can be applied alongside TDE, cell-level encryption and other obfuscation methods. One-way encryption is the topic of the next chapter.

CHAPTER 7: ONE-WAY ENCRYPTION

As a child, I often played the game of "guess what number I am thinking" with my friends. In this game, I would think of a number and only disclose the range of numbers in which the number resides. My friends would fire off a series of guesses until the secret number was guessed.

At a basic level one-way encryption is very similar. A secret value is encrypted and stored in a data table. However, unlike cell-level encryption, a key is not generated and so the cipher text that is created and stored remains in that protected state. Decryption does not occur with one-way encryption; thus the name of this method. Instead, you must hash the unencrypted value for which you are seeking and then compare it to the cipher text that is stored in the table.

A common use of one-way encryption is to protect passwords, messages, and it is sometimes used in digital signatures. However, it also can be used to protect sensitive data, such as credit card numbers, within the database. Some might argue that the suggestion to use one-way encryption to protect credit card details is near heresy, due to the vulnerabilities of one-way encryption to various forms of attack, such as dictionary or rainbow table attacks, and the potential for hash collisions.

In this chapter, we will explore these vulnerabilities in more detail and discuss how "salting" plain text will increase the complexity of the rendered hash value, and reduce the vulnerability to such attacks, along with the likelihood of hash collisions. We'll also investigate how use of other obfuscation methods, specifically truncation, can provide a solution to a real-world challenge that all encryption methods face.

In my opinion, one-way encryption is not the paper tiger that some make it out to be. Where there are weaknesses there are also ways to mitigate and strengthen, and one-way encryption should not be overlooked as a very valuable weapon in the battle to protect sensitive data.

How One-Way Encryption Works

As noted in the introduction, disclosure of the secret value, encrypted using one-way encryption, is achieved through comparing the stored hash value with a second hash value, or search value. This search value is generated using the same algorithm that created the stored hash value. When a positive match is verified between the stored hash value and the search value, the stored hash value's original plain text value is indirectly revealed, as illustrated in Figure 7-1.

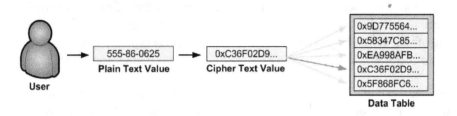

Figure 7-1: Searching for a plain text value among protected data.

In SQL Server, one-way encryption is accomplished through use of the Hashbytes method. This method uses a selected algorithm to generate a hash. Unlike the cell-level encryption methods, which produce a unique hash each time a plain text value is encrypted, the Hashbytes method will return the identical hash for a given text regardless to how many times the method is executed.

For example, when the plain text value of "1234567890" is hashed with the SHA1 algorithm, it will reliably return a hash value of 0x01B307ACBA4F54F55AAFC33BB06BBBF6CA803E9A each time Hashbytes is executed for that plain text value. Below is the syntax for this method:

```
HashBytes([Algorithm], [Plain Text])
```

This method's arguments are:

- **Algorithm**: The algorithm used to create the cipher text. The options for this argument are: MD2, MD4, MD5, SHA and SHA1. For specific details regarding these options see Chapter 4.

- **Plain Text**: The plain text that is being converted into cipher text.

The Hashbytes method will be used extensively in our implementation example of one-way encryption for our HomeLending database.

Benefits and Disadvantages of One-Way Encryption

In Chapter 5, we discussed the severe performance impact of searching on data that has been encrypted with cell-level encryption. While the strength of cell-level encryption and the granular level of control it provides to the security administrator are definite advantages, it limits the usability of some of the basic functionality of the database. One-way encryption is not as strong as cell-level encryption, but it does offer a layer of protection, while maintaining database and query performance.

As noted previously, there are many who will argue that one-way encryption should not be considered as an option to protect sensitive data due to its vulnerabilities and weaknesses. However, with a clear understanding of the benefits of the technique, its disadvantages, and the methods available to mitigate these disadvantages, some of the myths and warnings that exist regarding one-way encryption can be overcome.

This is not to say that one-way encryption is the answer for all of your sensitive data, or that it is so fool-proof. To determine if one-way encryption should be part of your protection efforts for sensitive data, consider the following benefits and disadvantages.

Benefits:

- **No key maintenance** – data that has been encrypted through one-way encryption is not decrypted; therefore there are no keys generated that require maintenance.

- **Negligible impact on database and query performance** – one-way encryption avoids the need to decrypt data, and uses a lightweight encryption algorithm, based on hash values. Please note that, optimally, any one-way encrypted field in a query should reside in the WHERE clause. If the plain text equivalent is presented in the SELECT clause, performance will be negatively affected.

Disadvantages:

- **Weaker algorithms** – the algorithms available for one-way encryption in SQL Server are considered weaker than the algorithms used in cell-level encryption or transparent data encryption.

- **May require schema modification** – the `Hashbytes` method returns a `varbinary` data type. Storage of this value, without conversion, will require a column of the same data type.

- **Security vulnerabilities of data in transit** – the `Hashbytes` method requires the passing of plain text into its arguments. This plain text value can be disclosed through using SQL Server Profiler, or any other database transaction monitoring tool.

Known Vulnerabilities

The Payment Card Industry Data Security Standard (PCI DSS), through requirement 3.4, does offer one-way encryption as a valid option in storing the primary account number, which is considered sensitive, in a database. The caveat is that the one-way encryption must use a strong algorithm. Among the algorithm options that are available to one-way encryption in SQL Server, PCI DSS defines the `SHA1` algorithm as being considered "... *an example of an industry-tested and accepted hashing algorithm.*", which is an acknowledgement that `SHA1` meets this criteria. For details regarding all of the algorithm options available with the `Hashbytes` method, see Chapter 4.

The following sections review a few of the most common known vulnerabilities, when using one-way encryption:

Dictionary Attack Vulnerability

A dictionary attack is one in which a list of values are hashed and then compared to the hash values stored in the target data table. This method is often used in an attempt to reveal passwords that are protected using one-way encryption.

By way of an example, consider an attempted dictionary attack is on the `Borrower_Identification` table of our `HomeLending` database, which we've protected using one-way encryption. Within the Identification_ Value column are the hash values of Social Security Numbers that are generated through one-way encryption.

The attack, depicted in Figure 7-2, is executed as follows:

- The attacker has created an "Attack Dictionary" of hash values that are based upon a sequence of plain text Social Security Numbers, ranging from "555-86-0622" through "555-86-0626".

- Each of the hash values in the attack dictionary is compared to the hash values stored in the Borrower_Identification table.

- A match is identified in the Borrower_Identification table with the attack hash value of 0xC36F02D9AC32B2E3813EFF9B 6C23D99D6038FD9A revealing that the plain text value of "555-86-0625" is a valid Social Security Number within the database.

- With this knowledge, the attacker gains access to associated information such as the borrower's name, address and birth date.

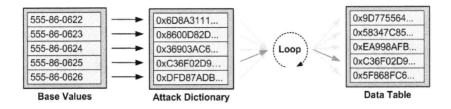

Figure 7-2: Dictionary Attack.

A dictionary attack takes advantage of the inherent nature of one-way encryption by performing the same action that is used when a user searches one-way encrypted data, but on a larger scale.

In our example, the attacker knows he is looking for Social Security Numbers which, in their plain text form, have a standard pattern. It is also known to the attacker that Social Security Numbers are commonly stored without the dash ("-") character. Therefore, the attacker has a finite set of base values that will likely return some matches.

If the DBA added a series of characters to the value of the Social Security Number, before it was encrypted, the resulting hash value would be different than the hash value resulting from encrypting the real Social Security Number, and would increase the number of possible character combinations required to return a positive match.

This process, called **salting** reduces the risk of a successful dictionary attack on the one-way encrypted values. Additional details regarding salting, as well as a specific example of using a salt with the HomeLending database, will be provided later in this chapter.

Rainbow Table Attack Vulnerability

Database Administrators are not the only people interested in efficiency. Those who are interested in attacking a database to reveal sensitive data that is protected through one-way encryption are also interested in the efficiency of their efforts. In order to initiate a dictionary attack on a database containing millions of records, the attacker would require a large attack dictionary to cover the possible combinations of plain text and hash values. This would result in a long running attack that requires a lot of resources from the database server, therefore increasing the risk of the attack being detected.

Therefore, the rainbow table attack was developed. The key player in this game is the **rainbow table**. The rainbow table consists of a series of rows holding two columns of data. The first column contains the plain text values that are being sought, for example a Social Security Number. The second column contains a value that is the ending hash of a **reduction chain**. A reduction chain is the result of taking the plain text value in the first column of our rainbow table and creating an **initial hash**; then, a portion of the initial hash, such as its first six digits, is obtained and another hash value is generated. This process continues for a number of iterations until an **ending hash** is derived.

The ending hash that is stored in the rainbow table represents an array of hash values that can be programmatically derived and iterated in an attack, through the reversal of the reduction chain building process. This approach provides a very efficient means of storing the seed values that are used to mount an attack on one-way encrypted data.

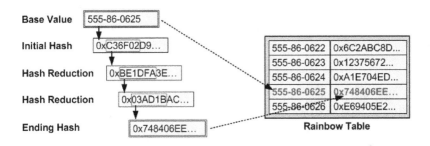

Figure 7-3: The creation of a rainbow table.

Let's consider an example of how this type of an attack can affect the sensitive data that is protected with one-way encryption. As before, we'll assume that a rainbow table attack is in progress on the `Borrower_Identification` table of our `HomeLending` database.

The attacker has created a rainbow table, with a reduction chain represented by each record's last link, based upon a sequence of plain text Social Security Numbers ranging from "555-86-0622" through "555-86-0626", as shown in Table 7-1.

Plain Text	Ending Hash in the Reduction Chain
555-86-0622	0x9AEE648230046F795612E1B04171F65CA164E4E1
555-86-0623	0x6CCCDD87AC087D7BDD92641EEF44635B6F4B7943
555-86-0624	0x8432814F76099E8EEE0BAA67F39CC44D5F254405
555-86-0625	0x277847607C4D9984C636628418FDFAEBA26B8B34
555-86-0626	0xE86571ACB27E193820DCEA9556F7556771F50D26

Table 7-1: The rainbow table.

Each of the final reduction chain link hash values in the rainbow table is compared to the hash values stored in the `Borrower_Identification` table. This step is basically identical to a dictionary attack. In our specific example, the result of this stage does not indicate a successful match for any of our ending hashes.

In the next stage of the attack, we revisit the process that created our ending hash: the chain reduction process. In our example, the reduction chain was generated based on the first six digits of each hash. In the execution of this attack we reverse the reduction chain by taking the first six digits of the hashed value that is the subject of our attack. Each subsequent link in the reversed reduction chain is compared to the ending hash that is stored in the rainbow table. In our case, a successful match occurs for the plain text value of "555-86-0625".

Much like a dictionary attack, a rainbow table attack can be reasonably mitigated through the use of a salt on your plain text, prior to applying the one-way encryption. These attacks rely on the perpetrator having anticipated a series of plain text values, hashing these values and then comparing the resulting hashes to the values stored within the database. The use of a salt increases the complexity of the plain text and reduces the likelihood that the anticipated value is among the plain text values sought by the attacker.

Additional details regarding salting, as well as a specific example of using a salt with the HomeLending database, will be provided later in this chapter.

Hash Collision Vulnerability

A hash collision occurs when two unique plain text values produce an identical hash value. An example would be both"555-86-1234" and "555-86-5298" returning the identical hash value. Since a value secured using one-way encryption is not decrypted, and its underlying plain text is revealed through the comparison of hash values, a hash collision presents a situation in which the actual plain text value cannot be determined.

The algorithm selected for the encryption process is critical in reducing the likelihood of hash collisions. Algorithms that produce lengthy hashes increase the array of possible values, and so reduce the probability of a hash collision.

Of course, the larger the volume of records to which these algorithms are applied, the higher is the risk of a hash collision. A mathematic problem called **"The Birthday Paradox"** is commonly referenced as a formula that can be used to determine the probability of hash collisions. While not specific to determining the probability of hash collisions, the Birthday Paradox formula can be modified to provide this information.

For those who are not mathematics or statistics majors, let's boil this issue down to its basics.

The possible unique combination of values for a single bit is 2 since a bit is either a 1 or a 0. The possible unique combination of values for a single byte, which is eight bits, would be 256, represented as 2^8. The algorithm options that are provided with one-way encryption return either a 128 bit or a 160 bit hash value. The possible unique combination of a 128 bit hash would be 340,282,36 6,920,938,460,000,000,000,000,000,000,000, represented as 2^{128}. The possible unique combination of a 160 bit hash would be 1,461,501,637,330,902,900,000 ,000,000,000,000,000,000,000,000,000, represented as 2^{160}.

In order for the possibilities of a hash collision to occur in the Identification_Value column of the Borrower_Identification table, using a 128 bit algorithm, to reach a meager 0.1% it would require a volume of 830,000,000,000,000,000,000 records; each containing a unique plain text value.

There are other factors that come into play that have influence on the actual possibilities of a hash collision, such as the internal processing that takes place within the algorithm. Regardless, the vulnerability for the occurrence of a hash collision is real and should be carefully considered.

With the selection of the hashing algorithm, inclusion of a salt prior to encryption, and by avoiding use of one-way encryption in tables that have an extremely high volume of rows, the potential vulnerabilities of the technique can be mitigated, and it becomes a worthy option to consider when protecting sensitive data.

Reducing Vulnerability: Salting a Hash

In culinary circles, salt is used as a preservative and a flavor enhancer. In the days before refrigeration meat was heavily salted for extended storage. The salt slowed the deterioration of the meat and prevented mold and bacteria from contaminating it. This protected the integrity of the meat so that its quality could be assured for a reasonable length of time.

Salt in cryptography has a similar effect. A one-way encrypted hash value is vulnerable to dictionary and rainbow table attacks; but adding a salt to the plain text, before it is encrypted, results in a hash value that is very resilient to these attacks. Salting renders the underlying plain text more complex, and breaks expected patterns that can be anticipated by the attacker.

For example, an attacker who is executing a dictionary attack against a table that contains unsalted hash values of Social Security Numbers will anticipate that the patterns of the plain text will be "000-00-0000" or "000000000". This known pattern provides the attacker with a finite combination of approximately one billion (10^9) possible values. However, if the Social Security Number is salted with a seven character alphanumeric value, for example, then the possible combinations for the plain text values skyrockets to over seventy eight quintillion (78×10^{18}). Therefore, salting is a highly effective way of strengthening one-way encryption.

In the `HomeLending` database we will create a scalar-valued user defined function, called `GetHashSalt`, which is designed to return a seven character value, which will be used as the salt portion of a one-way encryption process.

Scalar-valued user defined function:

… is a function in which the value that is returned from its execution is a single value.

Listing 7-1 shows the script to create our `GetHashSalt` function. We will offer six variations of salt values designated with the values "L01" through "L06". These variations will provide a deeper level of protection to items that are salted throughout our database. These are the values that will be passed through the `@Type` argument of this user defined function.

```
Use HomeLending;
GO

CREATE FUNCTION GetHashSalt
(
    @Type varchar(3)
)
RETURNS varchar(7)
WITH ENCRYPTION
AS
BEGIN

DECLARE @Rtn varchar(7)

IF @Type = 'L01' SET @Rtn = 'HYz5#45';
IF @Type = 'L02' SET @Rtn = 'Ku&7723';
IF @Type = 'L03' SET @Rtn = 'PW2%230';
IF @Type = 'L04' SET @Rtn = 'T^542Xc';
```

```
IF @Type = 'L05' SET @Rtn = '89*we@4';
IF @Type = 'L06' SET @Rtn = '098&tsS';

RETURN @Rtn;

END
GO
```

Listing 7-1: The GetHashSalt UDF.

Inclusion of the WITH ENCRYPTION option prevents the revelation of these salt values by viewing the definition of the user defined function, as well as preventing its modification. This renders the code of the user defined function invisible through catalog views, unencrypted backup files and through SSMS.

With this user defined function, we can salt our plain text values before they are encrypted. The process of doing this involves the following steps:

- **Call** the GetHashSalt user defined function and assign it to a variable.

- **Concatenate** the variable to the plain text of the data that is to be encrypted.

- **Place** the resulting concatenated value in the plain text argument of the Hashbytes function.

For example, an original plain text of "555-37-0143" and a salt value being "HYz5#4555", the resulting concatenated value will be "HYz5#45555-37-0143". Using the "SHA1" algorithm, the resulting salted hash value will be 0xD544F25AC44F6CBC108DA211D2A48990A343359C.

Listing 7-2 will grant EXECUTE permissions on the GetHashSalt UDF to the Sensitive_high and Sensitive_meduim database roles.

```
Use HomeLending;
GO

GRANT EXECUTE ON dbo.GetHashSalt
    TO Sensitive_high, Sensitive_medium;
GO
```

Listing 7-2: Granting permissions to the GetHashSalt UDF.

Specific examples of the application of a salt, with the HomeLending database, will be illustrated in the following one-way encryption demonstration.

Implementing One-Way Encryption

Using the HomeLending database, we will implement one-way encryption. For simplicity and clarity, we will focus on the Borrower_Identification table and we will assume that the modifications to the Borrower_Identification table and Identification_Value column, which were outlined in Chapter 5, either have been reversed through a backup file restore, or not implemented.

The steps we will follow are as follows:

1. **Always backup your database** prior to implementing any method of protection. Details regarding this process are covered in Chapter 6.

2. **Create the primary** varbinary hash column to store the hashed values of the Identification_Value column. This hashed column must only be accessible to members of the Sensitive_high database role.

3. **Create a secondary version of the hash column** that stores truncated hash values of the underlying plain text, in order that lower-privilege roles can still perform searches based on the values contained in the primary hash column.

4. **Salt the values** stored in the Identification_value column, using the GetSaltHash UDF created in Listing 7.1, and then hash the values, using the HashBytes method, and populate the hash columns.

5. **Test and verify** our new one-way encryption architecture.

6. **Drop the original plain-text** Identification_Value column.

These steps would be repeated, as needed, for each column in the database tables that are subject to the implementation of one-way encryption.

Please note that the process of implementing one-way encryption involves modification of existing database objects. Please perform a full database backup prior to proceeding in the event that recovery is required.

Create the Primary Hash Column

As noted in the review of the `Borrower_Identification` table in Chapter 5, the `Identification_Value` column contains the plain text representation of the actual identification value for a given borrower. For example, if the identification value was a Social Security Number, the value contained in this column would appear in the format of "555-55-5555".

The `Hashbytes` method that we'll use to one-way-encrypt our `Identification_Value` column returns a `varbinary` data type, which stores a variable-length numeric representation of a value. For example, the value of "A" is stored with the value of "0x41" while "ABC" is stored as "0x414243". The `varbinary` (and `Binary`) data type has a maximum length of 8,000 characters.

However, in the original schema design, the `Identification_Value` column is of data type `varchar`. Therefore, we will need to create a new column in the `HomeLending` database to store the encrypted `varbinary` values. Listing 7.3 shows the script to create a new `Identification_Value_H` column (where the "H" stands for hash) with the `varbinary` data type, using the `ALTER TABLE` method.

```
USE HomeLending;
GO

ALTER TABLE dbo.Borrower_Identification
    ADD Identification_Value_H varbinary(MAX) NULL;
GO
```

Listing 7-3: Creating the hash column.

In Listing 7-4, we execute the `sp_addextendedproperty` system stored procedure in order to document the fact that the new `Identification_Value_H` column is classified as "High" sensitivity.

```
USE HomeLending;
GO

EXEC sp_addextendedproperty
    @name='Sensitivity_Class',
    @value='High',
    @level0type='SCHEMA',
    @level0name='dbo',
    @level1type='TABLE',
    @level1name='Borrower_Identification',
```

```
    @level2type='COLUMN',
    @level2name='Identification_Value_H';
GO
```

Listing 7-4: Documenting the encrypted column as "high" sensitivity.

Create a Secondary Hash Column for Searching

With our HomeLending database, there is an expectation by the users that the members of the Sensitive_medium database role should be able to search for borrowers based upon the values contained in the Identification_Value column. However, our security policy dictates that the Identification_Value_H column has a Sensitivity_Class of "High", and so only members of the Sensitive_high database role are granted permissions to access it. This presents an interesting challenge.

A solution to this challenge is to offer an additional column that will contain the hash values of truncated versions of the original plain text. For example, this column would contain a hash of the last four digits of the Social Security Number. This new column will be offered to users who are not members of the Sensitive_high database role, as a way to search this data.

Listing 7-5 creates this new column, called Identification_Value_HT, on the Borrower_Identification table. The "T" represents the fact that it is a truncated version of the plain text value. In addition, we define its Sensitivity_Class designation as "Medium."

```
USE HomeLending;
GO

ALTER TABLE dbo.Borrower_Identification
    ADD Identification_Value_HT varbinary(MAX) NULL;
GO

EXEC sp_addextendedproperty
    @name='Sensitivity_Class',
    @value='Medium',
    @level0type='SCHEMA',
    @level0name='dbo',
    @level1type='TABLE',
    @level1name='Borrower_Identification',
    @level2type='COLUMN',
    @level2name='Identification_Value_HT';
GO
```

Listing 7-5: Creating and documenting the secondary hash column.

172

When we populate these new columns, the Identification_Value_H column will be populated with a hash value that is based on the full plain text value of the Identification_Value column, and the Identification_Value_HT column will be populated with a hash value that is based on the last four digits of the plain text. A salt will be applied to both, based upon our previously created GetHashSalt user defined function.

Populate the Hash Columns

The next step will be to populate our new Identification_Value_H and Identification_Value_HT columns with the hash values of the Identification_Value column.

Listing 7-6 shows the script to do this. It uses the GetHashSalt user defined function to salt the values in the Identification_Value column and then updates the data in our the newly-created hash columns in our Borrower_Identification table so that they are salted and hashed, in the case of the Identification_Value_H column, and salted, truncated and hashed, in the case of the Identification_Value_HT column.

```
USE HomeLending;
GO

DECLARE @Salt varchar(7)
SET @Salt = dbo.GetHashSalt('L01');

UPDATE dbo.Borrower_Identification
   SET Identification_Value_H =
         HASHBYTES('SHA1', @Salt +
            Identification_Value),
      Identification_Value_HT =
         HASHBYTES('SHA1', @Salt +
            RIGHT(Identification_Value,4));
GO
```

Listing 7-6: Salting and hashing the Identification_Value column.

Later in this chapter we will take the code provided in Listing 7-6 and place it in a stored procedure, which will be used when the records are inserted and updated.

Verify the Implementation

To verify that our hash values were successfully generated, we can execute SELECT statements that filter, based upon our newly generated columns, as shown in Listing 7-7.

```
USE HomeLending;
GO

DECLARE @Salt varchar(7)
SET @Salt = dbo.GetHashSalt('L01');

-- Returns search by full SSN
SELECT
   Identification_Value
FROM
   dbo.Borrower_Identification
WHERE
   Identification_Value_H =
        HASHBYTES('SHA1', @Salt + '555-20-7151');

-- Returns search by last four digits of SSN
SELECT
   Identification_Value
FROM
   dbo.Borrower_Identification
WHERE
   Identification_Value_HT =
        HASHBYTES('SHA1', @Salt + '7151');
GO
```

Listing 7-7: Testing the one-way encryption.

The results of these queries, indicating successful implementation of one-way encryption, would appear as follows:

```
Identification_Value
---------------------------------------------------------
555-20-7151
(1 row(s) affected)
Identification_Value
---------------------------------------------------------
555-20-7151
(1 row(s) affected)
```

Drop the Unencrypted Column

Having successfully encrypted the contents of our Identification_
Value column, captured it into the Identification_Value_H and
Identification_Value_HT columns, and verified that they are working
correctly; we can remove the Identification_Value column that
contains the plain text values of our sensitive data.

This is accomplished through the use of the ALTER TABLE method and the
DROP COLUMN argument, as shown in Listing 7-8.

```
USE HomeLending;
GO

ALTER TABLE dbo.Borrower_Identification
    DROP COLUMN Identification_Value;
GO
```

Listing 7-8: Dropping the plain-text column.

Please note that the plain text values contained in this column will be
permanently lost with its removal. This is definitely an action in which we
will want to take pause. Perform the DROP COLUMN command only if you are
certain that you will no longer need to reference its contents. At the beginning
of this process we performed a database backup which will provide us a means
of recovery if needed. If the plain text values are archived to another location it
too will need to be protected.

Creating the Interface

The sensitive data that is contained within the Borrower_Identification
table is now protected with one-way encryption. Our next steps are to create the
interface through which our users can access this table.

In Chapter 5, as a general policy, we denied direct access to all base tables
within the HomeLending database using the script shown in Listing 7-9.

```
USE HomeLending;
GO

DENY ALTER,CONTROL,REFERENCES,DELETE,INSERT,UPDATE,SELECT
    ON dbo.Borrower_Identification
```

```
        TO Sensitive_high, Sensitive_medium, Sensitive_low
  GO
```

Listing 7-9: Denying access to the base tables.

We adopt the same strategy here, using an interface consisting of a view and three stored procedures to mediate our users' interaction with this table. By implementing this structure we can control the access to our data at a more granular level than simply granting access to entire tables. In addition, this structure allows us the opportunity to embed cryptographic functionality and other logical methods into our views and stored procedures.

Creating the View

In Chapter 5, we created a view called vwBorrower_Identification, by which authorized users in the Sensitive_high and Sensitive_medium roles could access the values in the Borrower_Identification table (see Listing 5-13). However, only members of the Sensitive_high role were able to use this view to view in decrypted form the cell-level-encrypted values.

Here, we will recreate this view in light of our new one-way encryption architecture, as shown in Listing 7-10. Users of the view will not gain access to the Identification_Value_H column, so that the ability to reveal the plain text through comparison of hash values is limited to the database roles that are in the Sensitive_high database role. Instead, we include our alternative Identification_Value_HT column, which contains a hash value of the original plain text truncated to its last four digits.

```
USE HomeLending;
GO

-- Create the view
CREATE VIEW dbo.vwBorrower_Identification
AS

SELECT
    Borrower_Identification_ID,
    Borrower_ID,
    Identification_Type_ID,
        Identification_Value_HT
FROM
    dbo.Borrower_Identification;
GO
```

176

```
-- Grant Select Permissions
GRANT SELECT ON dbo.vwBorrower_Identification
    TO Sensitive_high, Sensitive_medium;
GO
```

Listing 7-10: Recreating the `vwBorrower_Identification` view.

Creating the Stored Procedures

Having earlier restricted direct access to the `Borrower_Identification` table, the ability to insert, update and search records that are contained within the `Borrower_Identification` table will be achieved through stored procedures.

The stored procedure that will be used to perform the UPDATE methods will be called `Update_Borrower_Identification` and the script to create it is shown in Listing 7-11. The plain text value of the borrower's identification value as well as the unique identifying value for the record that is being updated in the `Borrower_Identification` table is passed into this stored procedure as parameters. This stored procedure then performs the necessary salting and hashing, using the `GetHashSalt` function and the `Hashbytes` method, as described earlier.

```
USE HomeLending;
GO

CREATE PROCEDURE dbo.Update_Borrower_Identification
    @Borrower_Identification_ID bigint,
    @Identification_Value varchar(250)
AS
BEGIN TRY

    -- Get Salt
    DECLARE @Salt varchar(7)
    SET @Salt = dbo.GetHashSalt('L01');

    -- Performs the update of the record
    UPDATE dbo.Borrower_Identification
        SET Identification_Value_H =
                HashBytes('SHA1',@Salt +
                        @Identification_Value),
                Identification_Value_HT =
            HashBytes('SHA1',@Salt +
```

```
                          Right(@Identification_Value,4))
    WHERE
        Borrower_Identification_ID =
            @Borrower_Identification_ID;

END TRY
BEGIN CATCH
    -- Returns the error information
    SELECT
        ERROR_NUMBER() AS ErrorNumber,
        ERROR_SEVERITY() AS ErrorSeverity,
        ERROR_STATE() AS ErrorState,
        ERROR_MESSAGE() AS ErrorMessage;
END CATCH
GO
```

**Listing 7-11: Creating the `Update_Borrower_Identification`
stored procedure.**

The stored procedure that will be used to perform the INSERT methods will
be called `Insert_Borrower_Identification`. Passed into this stored
procedure as parameters are:

- The plain text value of the borrower's identification value.

- The foreign key value that defines the identification type.

- The foreign key value for the borrower to which the identification
  record is associated.

The script to create this stored procedure is shown in Listing 7-12.

```
USE HomeLending;
GO

CREATE PROCEDURE dbo.Insert_Borrower_Identification
    @Borrower_ID bigint,
    @Identification_Type_ID int,
    @Identification_Value varchar(250)
AS
BEGIN TRY

    -- Get Salt
    DECLARE @Salt varchar(7)
    SET @Salt = dbo.GetHashSalt('L01');

    -- Performs the update of the record
    INSERT INTO dbo.Borrower_Identification
```

```
        (
            Borrower_ID,
            Identification_Type_ID,
            Identification_Value_H,
            Identification_Value_HT
        )
        VALUES
        (
            @Borrower_ID,
            @Identification_Type_ID,
            HashBytes('SHA1',@Salt +
                        @Identification_Value),
            HashBytes('SHA1',@Salt +
                        Right(@Identification_Value,4))
        );

    -- Captures the new Borrower_Identifcation_ID value
    SELECT @@IDENTITY;

END TRY
BEGIN CATCH
    -- Returns the error information
    SELECT
        ERROR_NUMBER() AS ErrorNumber,
        ERROR_SEVERITY() AS ErrorSeverity,
        ERROR_STATE() AS ErrorState,
        ERROR_MESSAGE() AS ErrorMessage;
END CATCH
GO
```

**Listing 7-12: Creating the `Insert_Borrower_Identification`
stored procedure.**

Again, the `Hashbytes` method is used to create the hash value for the plain
text identification value and the salt is derived from the `GetHashSalt` user
defined function. The `SHA1` algorithm is used to create the hash value.

The final stored procedure, `Select_Borrower_Identification`, will be
used to return filtered sets of data based upon the truncated plain text, in this
case the last four digits, sent into its `Identification_Value` argument, as
shown in Listing 7-13.

```
USE HomeLending;
GO

CREATE PROCEDURE dbo.Search_Borrower_Identification
    @Identification_Value varchar(4)
```

```
AS
BEGIN TRY

    -- Get Salt
    DECLARE @Salt varchar(7)
    SET @Salt = dbo.GetHashSalt('L01');

    -- Return Search Results
    SELECT
        bn.Borrower_LName,
        bn.Borrower_FName,
        bn.Borrower_MName,
        bn.Borrower_Suffix
    FROM
        dbo.Borrower_Identification bi
        INNER JOIN dbo.Borrower_Name bn
            ON bi.Borrower_ID = bn.Borrower_ID
    WHERE
        bi.Identification_Value_HT =
            HashBytes('SHA1',@Salt +
                            @Identification_Value);

END TRY
BEGIN CATCH
    -- Returns the error information
    SELECT
        ERROR_NUMBER() AS ErrorNumber,
        ERROR_SEVERITY() AS ErrorSeverity,
        ERROR_STATE() AS ErrorState,
        ERROR_MESSAGE() AS ErrorMessage;
END CATCH
GO
```

**Listing 7-13: Creating the `Search_Borrower_Identification`
stored procedure.**

The plain text identification value that is passed in is salted and hashed, using
the "SHA1" algorithm, and then placed in the WHERE clause of the statement to
be compared with the hash value that is stored in the table.

Setting and Verifying Permissions to the Stored Procedures

Once the stored procedures have been created, we need to grant the appropriate permissions to them (see Listing 7-14). With the HomeLending database we will be operating on the assumption that the Sensitive_high database role will have access to the information that will be inserted and updated to the Borrower_Identification table.

The ability to search the data that is in the Borrower_Identification table will be granted to the Sensitive_high and Sensitive_medium database roles, due to our use of the Identification_Value_HT column that contains a hash value of the last four digits of our original plain text.

```
USE HomeLending;
GO

-- Grant Execute Permissions to Sensitive_high database
role
GRANT EXECUTE ON dbo.Update_Borrower_Identification
    TO Sensitive_high;
GO

-- Grant Execute Permissions to Sensitive_high database
role
GRANT EXECUTE ON dbo.Insert_Borrower_Identification
    TO Sensitive_high;
GO

-- Grant Execute Permissions to Sensitive_high
-- and Sensitive_medium database roles
GRANT EXECUTE ON dbo.Search_Borrower_Identification
    TO Sensitive_high, Sensitive_medium;
GO
```

Listing 7-14: Setting permissions to the stored procedures.

Now that our stored procedures have been created we will want to verify that the permissions are effective, using of EXECUTE AS USER to impersonate a member of the various database roles. The use of REVERT terminates the impersonation and returns us to our original user account.

Listing 7-15 executes the Search_Borrower_Identification stored procedure with the plain text value of "0143", which is the last four digits of a known Social Security Number, being passed as its argument.

```
USE HomeLending;
GO

-- execute as a user who is a member of Sensitive_high role
EXECUTE AS USER = 'WOLFBA';
GO
Exec dbo.Search_Borrower_Identification '0143';
GO
REVERT;
GO

-- execute as a user who is a member of Sensitive_medium
role

EXECUTE AS USER = 'KELLEYWB';
GO
Exec dbo.Search_Borrower_Identification '0143';
GO
REVERT;
GO

-- execute as a user who is a member of Sensitive_low role
EXECUTE AS USER = 'JONESBF';
GO
Exec dbo.Search_Borrower_Identification '0143';
GO
REVERT;
GO
```

Listing 7-15: Verifying permissions.

The result of this verification will reflect that rows were returned for the queries for the Sensitive_high and Sensitive_medium members; but since permissions did not exist for the Sensitive_low members the actual rows will not be returned. Instead the following will appear:

```
(1 row(s) affected)
(1 row(s) affected)
Msg 229, Level 14, State 5, Line 1
The EXECUTE permission was denied on the object 'Search_
Borrower_Identification', database 'HomeLending', schema
'dbo'.
```

To view the actual rows returned, execute each batch in this script individually.

Summary

Through this demonstration we have successfully implemented one-way encryption for the `Borrower_Identification` table of our `HomeLending` database. This addresses only the plain text in a single column of a single table. Within the database there are many more columns that may be good candidates for one-way encryption.

Through our exploration of the various attacks that can be waged against data that is protected with one-way encryption, and our better understanding of the potential for hash collisions, we have a better understanding of when the option to apply one-way encryption is valid and when it is not.

The addition of a salt through the use of the `GetHashSalt` user defined function provided additional strength to our hash values and mitigated its vulnerabilities to attack; widening the opportunity to use this valuable feature to protect our sensitive data while maintaining functionality that is lost with other encryption methods.

Now that we have a cell-level encryption, transparent data encryption and one-way encryption available to us in our sensitive data protection efforts, let's proceed in considering other obfuscation methods that do not require encryption.

CHAPTER 8: OBFUSCATION

Halloween is one of my favorite times of the year. On this holiday, the young and young at heart apply make-up, masks, costumes and outfits and wander the streets in search of sweet treats from their neighbors. These costumes are designed to hide the identity of their wearer and grant that person the freedom to shed their everyday demeanor and temporarily adopt the persona of their disguise.

Applying the technique of obfuscation to our sensitive data is somewhat akin to donning a Halloween disguise. By doing so, we mask the underlying data values, hiding their true nature, until the appropriate time to disclose it.

The previous chapters have explored in detail various encryption techniques, all of which are considered forms of obfuscation. In this chapter, we will explore a handful of additional obfuscation techniques, which do not require an algorithm, encryption key, decryption key or transformation of data types.

Each of these methods, including character scrambling and masking, numeric variance and nulling, rely on an array of built-in SQL Server system functions that are used for string manipulation.

While these methods of obfuscation will not be used by any federal government to protect nuclear missile launch codes, they can be highly effective when printing documents that contain sensitive data, transferring production data to test environments or presenting data through reporting and warehousing mechanisms.

Development Environment Considerations

Before we proceed with an exploration of obfuscation methods, let's spend a few moments reviewing a strong candidate for the implementation of the obfuscation methods presented in this chapter: the *development* environment.

The database that is utilized for daily business transactions is referred to as the production database. The version of the database that is used to develop and test new functionality is referred to as the development database. These environments are separated so that new development and troubleshooting can

185

occur without having a negative effect on the performance and integrity of the production database.

Any proposed modifications to a production database should be first implemented and tested on a development or test database. In order to ensure the accuracy of this testing, the development database should mimic the production database as closely as possible, in terms of the data it contains and the set of security features it implements.

This means that all of the sensitive data efforts and options noted in this book apply to both environments and that it may be necessary to store sensitive data in both the development and production databases. The difficulty with this is that it is common for developers and testers to be granted elevated permissions within the development database. If the development database contains identical data to that stored in the production database, then these elevated permissions could present a severe and intolerable security risk to the organization and its customers.

In order to mitigate this risk, the Database Administrator responsible for refreshing the contents of the development environment should apply obfuscation methods to hide the actual values that are gleaned from the production environment.

Obfuscation Methods

The word *obfuscation* is defined by the American Heritage Dictionary as follows:

> *"To make so confused or opaque as to be difficult to perceive or understand ... to render indistinct or dim; darken."*

The word obfuscation, at times, can be used interchangeably with the term obscurity, meaning "*the quality or condition of being unknown*". However, there is a subtle difference between the two terms and the former definition is more appropriate since obscurity implies that the hidden condition can be achieved without any additional effort.

Many methods of "disguise", or obfuscation, are available to the Database Administrator that can contribute a level of control to how sensitive data is stored and disclosed, in both production and development environments. The options that will be discussed in this chapter are:

- Character Scrambling
- Repeating Character Masking
- Numeric Variance
- Nulling
- Artificial Data Generation
- Truncating
- Encoding
- Aggregating.

Many of these methods rely on SQL Server's built-in system functions for string manipulation, such as SUBSTRING, REPLACE, and REPLICATE. Appendix A provides a syntax reference for these, and other system functions that are useful in obfuscating sensitive data.

Prior to diving into the details of these obfuscation methods we need to explore the unique value of another system function, called RAND.

The Value of RAND

The RAND system function is not one that directly manipulates values for the benefit of obfuscation, but its ability to produce a reasonably random value makes it a valuable asset when implementing character scrambling or producing a numeric variance.

One special consideration of the RAND system function is that when it is included in a user defined function an error will be returned when the user defined function is created.

```
Msg 443, Level 16, State 1, Procedure SampleUDF, Line 12
Invalid use of a side-effecting operator 'rand' within a
function.
```

This can be overcome by creating a view that contains the RAND system function and referencing the view in the user defined function. The script in

Listing 8-1 will create a view in the HomeLending database that returns a random value, using the RAND system function. Since this view holds no security threat, we will make this available to the Sensitive_high, Sensitive_medium and Sensitive_low database roles with SELECT permissions on this view.

```
Use HomeLending;
GO

-- Used to reference RAND with in a function
CREATE VIEW dbo.vwRandom
AS
SELECT RAND() as RandomValue;
GO

-- Grant permissions to view
GRANT SELECT ON dbo.vwRandom
    TO Sensitive_high, Sensitive_medium, Sensitive_low;
GO
```

Listing 8-1: Generating random numbers using RAND .

Now, we can obtain a random number in any user defined function with a simple call to our new view. In Listing 8-2, an example is provided that produces a random number between the values of 1 and 100.

```
DECLARE @Rand float;
DECLARE @MinVal int;
DECLARE @MaxVal int;
SET @MinVal = 1;
SET @MaxVal = 100;

SELECT
    @Rand = ((@MinVal + 1) - @MaxVal) * RandomValue + @
MaxVal
FROM
    dbo.vwRandom;
GO
```

Listing 8-2: Testing the View.

Appendix A of this book provides a syntax reference for the RAND system function.

Character Scrambling

Character scrambling is a process by which the characters contained within a given statement are re-ordered in such a way that its original value is obfuscated. For example, the name "Jane Smith" might be scrambled into "nSem Jatih".

This option does have its vulnerabilities. The process of cracking a scrambled word is often quite straightforward, and indeed is a source of entertainment for many, as evidenced by newspapers, puzzle publications and pre-movie entertainment.

Cracking a scrambled word can be made more challenging by, for example, eliminating any repeating characters and returning only lower case letters. However, not all values will contain repeating values, so this technique may not be sufficient for protecting highly sensitive data.

The Character Scrambling UDF

In the HomeLending database we will create a user defined function called Character_Scramble that performs character scrambling, which is shown in Listing 8-3. It will be referenced as needed in views and stored procedures that are selected to use this method of data obfuscation.

Included in this user defined function is a reference to the vwRandom view that was created in Listing 8-1. In essence, this user defined function will loop through all of the characters of the value that is passed through the @OrigVal argument replacing each character with other randomly selected characters from the same string. For example, the value of "John" may result as "nJho".

In order for the appropriate users to utilize this user defined function permissions must be assigned. The GRANT EXECUTE command is included in the following script.

```
Use HomeLending;
GO

-- Create user defined function
CREATE FUNCTION Character_Scramble
(
    @OrigVal varchar(max)
)
```

189

```
RETURNS varchar(max)
WITH ENCRYPTION
AS
BEGIN

-- Variables used
DECLARE @NewVal varchar(max);
DECLARE @OrigLen int;
DECLARE @CurrLen int;
DECLARE @LoopCt int;
DECLARE @Rand int;

-- Set variable default values
SET @NewVal = '';
SET @OrigLen = DATALENGTH(@OrigVal);
SET @CurrLen = @OrigLen;
SET @LoopCt = 1;

-- Loop through the characters passed
WHILE @LoopCt <= @OrigLen
    BEGIN
        -- Current length of possible characters
        SET @CurrLen = DATALENGTH(@OrigVal);

        -- Random position of character to use
        SELECT
            @Rand = Convert(int,(((1) - @CurrLen) *
                               RandomValue + @CurrLen))
        FROM
            dbo.vwRandom;

        -- Assembles the value to be returned
        SET @NewVal = @NewVal +
                               SUBSTRING(@OrigVal,@Rand,1);

        -- Removes the character from available options
        SET @OrigVal =
                Replace(@OrigVal,SUBSTRING(@OrigVal,@
Rand,1),'');

        -- Advance the loop
        SET @LoopCt = @LoopCt + 1;
    END
    -- Returns new value
    Return LOWER(@NewVal);
```

```
END
GO


-- Grant permissions to user defined function
GRANT EXECUTE ON dbo.Character_Scramble
    TO Sensitive_high, Sensitive_medium, Sensitive_low;
GO
```

Listing 8-3: The character scrambling UDF.

This user defined function takes advantage of system functions such as DATALENGTH which provides the length of a value, SUBSTRING which is used to obtain a portion of a value, REPLACE which replaces a value with another value and LOWER which returns the value in lowercase characters. All are valuable to string manipulation. Appendix A of this book provides a syntax reference regarding these system functions.

This UDF will be referenced in any views and stored procedures that are selected to use this method of data obfuscation, an example of which we'll see in the next section.

Repeating Character Masking

Over recent years the information that is presented on a credit card receipt has changed. In the past, it was not uncommon to find the entire primary account number printed upon the receipt. Today, this number still appears on credit card receipts; but only a few of the last numbers appear in plain text with the remainder of the numbers being replaced with a series of "x" or "*" characters. This is called a **repeating character mask**.

This approach provides a level of protection for sensitive data, rendering it useless for transactional purposes, while providing enough information, the number's last four digits, to identify the card on which the transaction was made.

In the HomeLending database, we will create a user defined function called Character_Mask, as shown in Listing 8-4, which performs repeating character masking, which again can be referenced as needed in views and stored procedures that are selected to use this method of data obfuscation.

This user defined function will modify the value that is passed through the @OrigVal argument and replace all of the characters with the character passed

through the @MaskChar argument. The @InPlain argument
defines the number of characters that will remain in plain text after this
user defined function is executed. For example, the value of "Samsonite" may
result in "xxxxxxite".

In order for the appropriate users to utilize this user defined function
permissions must be assigned. The GRANT EXECUTE command is included in
the script.

```
Use HomeLending;
GO

-- Create user defined function
CREATE FUNCTION Character_Mask
(
    @OrigVal varchar(max),
    @InPlain int,
    @MaskChar char(1)
)
RETURNS varchar(max)
WITH ENCRYPTION
AS
BEGIN

    -- Variables used
    DECLARE @PlainVal varchar(max);
    DECLARE @MaskVal varchar(max);
    DECLARE @MaskLen int;

    -- Captures the portion of @OrigVal that remains in
plain text
    SET @PlainVal = RIGHT(@OrigVal,@InPlain);
    -- Defines the length of the repeating value for the
mask
    SET @MaskLen = (DATALENGTH(@OrigVal) - @InPlain);
    -- Captures the mask value
    SET @MaskVal = REPLICATE(@MaskChar, @MaskLen);
    -- Returns the masked value
    Return @MaskVal + @PlainVal;

END
GO

-- Grant permissions to user defined function
```

```
GRANT EXECUTE ON dbo.Character_Mask
    TO Sensitive_high, Sensitive_medium, Sensitive_low;
GO
```

Listing 8-4: The `Character_Mask` UDF.

This user defined function takes advantage of system functions such as
DATALENGTH, which provides the length of a value, and REPLICATE which
is used to repeat a given character for a defined number of iterations. Both of
these are valuable to string manipulation.

NOTE:

Appendix A of this book provides a syntax reference regarding these
system functions.

To illustrate the use of this, and our previous Character_Scramble user
defined function, to present data in a masked format to the user, we will create
a view in the HomeLending database, called vwLoanBorrowers, for the
members of the Sensitive_high and Sensitive_medium database roles.

This view, shown in Listing 8-5, will present to the lender case numbers, using
the Character_Mask user defined function, and the borrower names using
the Character_Scramble user defined function.

```
Use HomeLending;
GO

CREATE VIEW dbo.vwLoanBorrowers
AS
SELECT
    dbo.Character_Mask(ln.Lender_Case_Number,4,'X')
        AS Lender_Case_Number,
    dbo.Character_Scramble(bn.Borrower_FName + ' '
        + bn.Borrower_LName)
        AS Borrower_Name
FROM
    dbo.Loan ln
    INNER JOIN dbo.Loan_Borrowers lb
        ON ln.Loan_ID = lb.Loan_ID
        AND lb.Borrower_Type_ID = 1 -- Primary Borrowers
Only
    INNER JOIN dbo.Borrower_Name bn
```

```
          ON lb.Borrower_ID = bn.Borrower_ID;
GO

-- Grant permissions to view
GRANT SELECT ON dbo.vwLoanBorrowers
    TO Sensitive_high, Sensitive_medium;
GO
```

Listing 8-5: The vwLoanBorrowers View.

The vwLoanBorrowers view, without the use of the masking user defined functions, would have returned the data set shown in Table 8-1.

Lender Case Number	Borrower Name
9646384387HSW	Damion Booker
8054957254EZE	Danny White

Table 8-1: The non-obfuscated result set.

However, with the user defined functions in place the masked data set shown in Table 8-2 is returned:

Lender Case Number	Borrower Name
XXXXXXXXX7HSW	o akdenbimr
XXXXXXXXX4EZE	ni ahtydwe

Table 8-2: The results returned after character masking and scrambling.

Numeric Variance

Numeric variance is a process in which the numeric values that are stored within a development database can be changed, within a defined range, so as not to reflect their actual values within the production database. By defining a percentage of variance, say within 10% of the original value, the values remain realistic for development and testing purposes. The inclusion of a randomizer to the percentage that is applied to each row will prevent the disclosure of the actual value, through identification of its pattern.

In the HomeLending database, we will create a user defined function called Numeric_Variance that increases or decreases the value of the value passed to it by some defined percent of variance, also passed as a parameter to the

194

function. For example, if we want the value to change within 10% of its current value we would pass the value of 10 in the @ValPercent argument.

A randomizer is added through the use of the vwRandom view that we created earlier in this chapter. This will vary the percent variance on a per execution basis. For example, the first execution may change the original value by 2%, while the second execution may change it by 6%.

The script to create this Numeric_Variance function, which can be referenced as needed in other views and stored procedures, is shown in Listing 8-6.

```
USE HomeLending;
GO

-- Create user defined function
CREATE FUNCTION Numeric_Variance
(
    @OrigVal float,
    @VarPercent numeric(5,2)
)
RETURNS float
WITH ENCRYPTION
AS
BEGIN
    -- Variable used
    DECLARE @Rand int;

    -- Random position of character to use
    SELECT
        @Rand = Convert(int,((((0-@VarPercent)+1) -
                @VarPercent) * RandomValue + @VarPercent))
    FROM
        dbo.vwRandom;

    RETURN @OrigVal + CONVERT(INT,((@OrigVal*@Rand)/100));
END
GO

-- Grant permissions to user defined function
GRANT EXECUTE ON dbo.Numeric_Variance
    TO Sensitive_high, Sensitive_medium, Sensitive_low;
GO
```

Listing 8-6: The **Numeric_Variance** UDF.

195

To employ this method of masking in a development database, simply use an UPDATE statement to change the column's value to a new value, using our Numeric_Variance function, as shown in Listing 8-7.

```
USE HomeLending;
GO

-- Variables used
DECLARE @Variance numeric(5,2)
-- Set variance to 10%
SET @Variance = 10

UPDATE dbo.Loan_Term
    SET Loan_Amount =
            dbo.Numeric_Variance(Loan_Amount,@Variance)
FROM
    dbo.Loan_Term;
GO
```

Listing 8-7: Updating a development database to use numeric variance.

Nulling

The process of nulling is the replacement of sensitive data with a NULL value, thus rendering the sensitive data unavailable in the development database. While this certainly protects the sensitive data, since the values are no longer known in the database, it does present issues if there are dependencies upon this data or constraints that do not permit a NULL value. Also, use of nulling can also present difficulties when trying to troubleshoot issues that specifically involve sensitive data.

To employ this method of masking in a development database, simply use an UPDATE statement to set the column's value to NULL, as shown in Listing 8-8.

```
USE HomeLending;
GO

UPDATE dbo.Borrower_Identification
    SET Identification_Value = NULL
FROM
    dbo.Borrower_Identification;
GO
```

Listing 8-8: Nulling a database column.

Truncation

Truncation is a method of protecting sensitive data where a portion of its value is removed. The concept is very similar to the repeating character masking covered earlier except that rather than replacing values with a "mask", such as an "x" or "*", truncating simply discards those values. For example, a Social Security Number, "555-86-1234", that is stored in plain text might be truncated to the value of "1234".

One way to apply this method is to permanently modify the stored value in the database by executing an UPDATE statement using the LEFT, RIGHT or SUBSTRING system function to define the remaining portion of the value.

For example, the script in Listing 8-9 uses the LEFT function to truncate all but the last four digits from the Identification_Value column.

```
USE HomeLending;
GO

UPDATE dbo.Borrower_Identification
    SET Identification_Value =
            LEFT(Identification_Value,4)
FROM
    dbo.Borrower_Identification;
GO
```

Listing 8-9: Permanently truncating the `Identification_Value` column.

Alternatively, in order to maintain the original value but perform the truncation for viewing, we can simply reference the column in views and stored procedures that use the LEFT, RIGHT or SUBSTRING system functions to define the remaining portion of the value. For example, Listing 8-10 returns only the last four digits of the values of the Identification_ Value column.

```
USE HomeLending;
GO

SELECT
    LEFT(Identification_Value,4) AS Identification_Value
FROM
    dbo.Borrower_Identification;
GO
```

Listing 8-10: Returning a truncated value.

Encoding

Encoding is a technique in which a series of characters is used to represent another value. This technique can be used to camouflage sensitive data, since the code used has no meaning outside the system in which the code is defined.

NOTE:

There are many benefits to encoding, beyond securing sensitive data, such as overcoming language barriers when working in an international environment and providing an expedient means of entering data.

Encoding is a practice that is found in abundance in the health care industry. The World Health Organization maintains the International Classification of Diseases (ICD), which is an industry standard that defines codes that represent diseases and health problems. These codes are used in health records and death certificates. For example, the ICD code for bacterial pneumonia is J15.9.

In the establishment of foreign keys in the HomeLending database we have, at a basic level, implemented encoding. The Loan table, for example, contains two columns that are named Purpose_Type_ID and Mortgage_Type_ID as illustrated in Figure 8-1 (for a full representation of the HomeLending schema, see Figure 2-1, in Chapter 2).

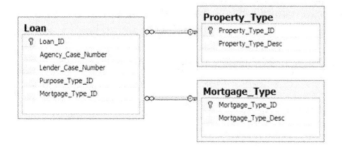

Figure 8-1: Loan table with Foreign Key Relationships

The Purpose_Type_ID and Mortgage_Type_ID columns are foreign keys to the Purpose_Type table and Mortgage_Type table. These tables contain, respectively, the list of potential purposes for a loan and the types of available mortgage, as defined in the Uniform Residential Loan Application, developed by the Federal National Mortgage Association, commonly known as Fannie Mae.

In the `Purpose_Type` table, we have used a sequence of numbers to indicate these purposes. So, for example, when a new loan record is created, the value of "2" is captured instead of the value "Refinance".

To further enhance this encoding, we may choose to either utilize a higher starting number in our sequence, such as "5,000", so that the options can be organized into logical groups. For example, we may have various types of refinance options for our borrowers. Through a higher starting number we could use the value range of 5,000 through 5,100 to represent the available refinance options, while construction loans might be found in the 2,000 through 2,100 range.

Aggregation

Aggregation is a technique in which identifying details of data are obfuscated through its provision in a summarized format. A few examples of presenting data as an aggregation are as follows:

- **As an average**: 40% of the loans originated in the `HomeLending` database during the past quarter were refinance loans.

- **As a calculated sum**: $2.5 million in loans were originated in the `HomeLending` during the past quarter.

- **As a geographical statistic**: The median home value in the city of Indianapolis, Indiana is $150,000.

Aggregating is a common technique used to populate data warehouses for data analysis. This not only protects the underlying sensitive data, but also reduces the storage requirements for the data.

An advantage of this approach is that the data that is provided to the user is only that which they need for their reporting and analysis requirements, so the potential for the leakage of sensitive data is greatly reduced.

A disadvantage to this approach is that if the aggregations are determined to be inaccurate, the detail data is not available to identify the cause. Another challenge to this approach is that a given aggregation may not meet everyone's needs, resulting in requests for different views of the same aggregated data, which increases your maintenance footprint.

Within the `HomeLending` database, aggregation may be beneficial in the collection of the borrower's liabilities. The current design of the `Borrower_ Liability` table requires the capture of the monthly payment amount and remaining balance. As shown in Figure 8-2, the `Borrower_Liability` table is related to the `Liability_Account` table, which reveals the creditor and account number of the liability.

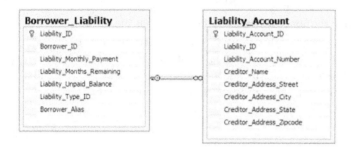

Figure 8-2: The `Borrower_Liability` and `Liability_Account` Tables.

An alternate approach would be to dispose of the `Liability_Account` table and simply capture a single record for the loan application, indicating the sum of their monthly payments and remaining balances for all liabilities, as shown in Figure 8-3.

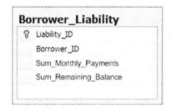

Figure 8-3: Alternate approach for `Borrower_Liability` table.

This level of detail would suffice for most users of this database and would protect this sensitive information from being inappropriately disclosed. The Underwriters, who may need access to the detailed liability data for qualification purposes, would refer to the credit report data, which is stored in a separate database, to determine whether or not the borrower can be approved for the loan.

Artificial Data Generation

As an alternative to these obfuscating techniques, you can generate data using third party tools, such as Red Gate's SQL Data Generator, which can produce large volumes of artificial data, based upon regular expressions and predefined ranges of values.

This provides protection of sensitive data due to the artificial nature of the data that is generated. In many cases, these third party tools will not execute internal encryption and obfuscation methods. This should not discourage the consideration of artificial data generation. This is noted simply to note that you may need to consider these special methods in a separate process from the general artificial data generation process.

Summary

In this chapter, we explored some options that are available to protect sensitive data through obfuscation. The system functions that are available in SQL Server provide us with the tools that can be employed in our views, stored procedures and user defined functions to create an effective line of defense.

Once our sensitive data has been secured we will want to identify when an attacker has gained access to our system and is snooping around for sensitive data. In addition, we will want to identify when valid users of our database are taking actions that may be suspicious. This can be done through the auditing feature of SQL Server 2008, and through a practice known as honeycombing.

CHAPTER 9: HONEYCOMBING A DATABASE

In the world of network servers, the term "honeypot" refers to a server that is placed in an environment for the sole purpose of attracting those who are snooping around, and capturing their activities within the honeypot server.

Honeycombing a database is a very similar approach and involves creating "decoy" tables within a database that appear to contain valid, and unprotected, sensitive data. When unauthorized activity occurs on the decoy table, it is captured in an audit table and a notification is sent to the appropriate parties.

Once the notification is received by the Database Administrator, immediate termination of the violating user account can occur. Also, the data that is captured during the unauthorized activity can be reviewed to gain a better understanding of how unauthorized activities are occurring and identify ways to prevent them from occurring on the real data.

Until the release of SQL Server 2008, the process of honeycombing a SQL Server database was very difficult. Triggers could be used to capture the occurrences of UPDATE, INSERT and DELETE statements; but nothing was available to capture SELECT statements, beyond running SQL Server Profiler. With SQL Server 2008's auditing feature, a much wider array of events, including SELECT statements, are available, with the added advantage that we don't need to use triggers to capture these events.

This chapter will demonstrate how to create a honeycomb table, audit activity on it, and send notifications of this activity to the relevant parties.

Implementing a Honeycomb Table

The process of honeycombing a database begins with the creation of a decoy table. The script in Listing 9-1 creates a honeycomb table in the default Database Object Schema of our HomeLending database. It has the mouthwatering name of Customer_Information and the column names, including First_Name, Social_Security_Number and Address_Street, are equally likely to attract the attention of the data thief.

203

```
Use HomeLending;
GO

CREATE TABLE dbo.Customer_Information
(
    Customer_ID bigint IDENTITY(100,1) NOT NULL,
    First_Name varchar(50) NOT NULL,
    Last_Name varchar(50) NOT NULL,
    Social_Security_Number varchar(12) NOT NULL,
    Address_Street varchar(250) NOT NULL,
    Address_City varchar(150) NOT NULL,
    Address_State varchar(2) NOT NULL,
    Address_Zipcode varchar(10) NOT NULL
);
GO
```

Listing 9-1: The `Customer_Information` Honeycomb table.

One of the goals in honeycombing a database is to capture the casual exploration of data by users who have limited authorized access to the database. To open this decoy table to all levels of curiosity, we will grant SELECT, INSERT, UPDATE and DELETE permissions to the public database role, using the GRANT statement, as shown in Listing 9-2. All database users are members of the public database role by default.

```
Use HomeLending;
GO

GRANT SELECT, INSERT, UPDATE, DELETE
    ON dbo.Customer_Information
    TO public;
GO
```

Listing 9-2: Open season on the Honeycomb table.

Simply having an empty decoy table in your database will not be sufficient to draw activity its way. It must be filled with alluring, but bogus, data. The first rule in populating this decoy table is obviously never to use actual data.

Data scrambling techniques can be applied, as described in Chapter 8, or you can generate decoy data using a data generator, such as Red Gate's SQL Data Generator. It is recommended that you populate the decoy table with a number of rows that is consistent with the non-decoy tables. In our HomeLending database, SQL Data Generator was used to populate five thousand rows of data, a sample of which are shown in Figure 9-1.

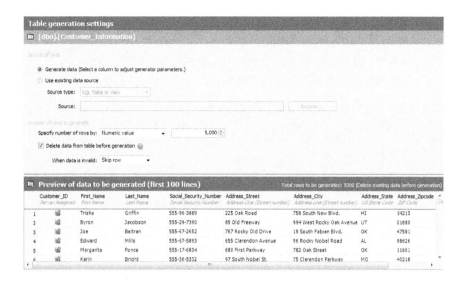

Figure 9-1: Screenshot from Red Gate's SQL Data Generator.

Creating a Server Audit

In order to capture the activity of would-be data thieves on our honeycomb table, we need to implement the auditing feature of SQL Server 2008. The first step in this process is to create a `Server Audit` object, which allows us to monitor a collection of actions that might occur on the target table, and record this activity in a file, typically the Windows Application log file.

The syntax of the `CREATE SERVER AUDIT` method is as follows:

```
CREATE SERVER AUDIT [Audit Name] TO [Output Location]
```

The arguments to this method are:

- **Audit Name** – the textual reference to the server audit.
- **Output Location** – the options for this argument are:

- **FILE**: write to a binary file. The file path is required in parenthesis after "File" is specified.
- **APPLICATION_LOG**: write to the Windows Application Log.
- **SECURITY_LOG**: write to the Windows Security Log.

In Listing 9-3, we create in the Master database a Server Audit object called Honeycomb_Audit, which will write to the Windows Application Log.

```
USE Master;
GO

CREATE SERVER AUDIT Honeycomb_Audit
    TO APPLICATION_LOG;
GO
```

Listing 9-3: Creating the Server Audit object.

Note that the Server Audit object is created at the instance level so the reference to the database in which the method was executed is not required.

When a Server Audit is created, it is disabled by default and will need to be enabled in order for it to begin collecting information. Listing 9-4 activates the Server Audit.

```
USE Master;
GO

ALTER SERVER AUDIT Honeycomb_Audit
WITH (STATE = ON);
GO
```

Listing 9-4: Activating the Honeycomb_Audit.

Creating a Database Audit Specification

A Database Audit Specification is a member of the Server Audit and collects specific information about the database-level events on which the Server Audit reports. The CREATE DATABASE AUDIT SPECIFICATION method is executed in SSMS to create a Database Audit Specification. The following is an example of the syntax of this method:

```
CREATE DATABASE AUDIT SPECIFICATION [Specification
Name]
    FOR [Server Audit]
    ADD ([Action] ON [Securable] BY [Principal])
    WITH (STATE = {ON|OFF})
```

The arguments to this method are:

- **Specification Name** – the textual reference to the Database Audit Specification.

- **Server Audit** – the textual reference to the Server Audit of which the Database Audit Specification is a member.

- **Action** – the action or comma delimited list of actions to be monitored.

- **Securable** – the database object that is to be monitored.

- **Principal** – the Database User, Database Role, or Application Role that is being monitored.

- **With State** – defines whether the Database Audit Specification is active (ON) or inactive (OFF).

In the HomeLending database, we will create a Database Audit Specification with the name of Customer_Information_Spec and capture any SELECT, INSERT, UPDATE and DELETE events that are performed by the public database role, as shown in Listing 9-5.

```
Use HomeLending;
GO

CREATE DATABASE AUDIT SPECIFICATION Customer_Information_
Spec
    FOR SERVER AUDIT Honeycomb_Audit
    ADD (SELECT, UPDATE, INSERT, DELETE
        ON dbo.Customer_Information
        BY public)
    WITH (STATE = ON);
GO
```

Listing 9-5: Creating the Database Audit Specification object.

All database users are members of the public database role; therefore we will know when any user executes any of these methods on our decoy table.

Reviewing the Windows Application Log

By executing a simple SELECT statement against our decoy table, in the HomeLending database, the Server Audit is initiated. Many pieces of information are captured in the Windows Application Log, but the most critical in identifying the event that occurred are shown in Table 9-1.

Log Item	Captured Value	Description
Source:	MSSQL$SQLINSTANCEA	The Instance Name
Date:	5/28/2009 6:16:30 AM	The Time of the Event
Keywords:	Classic,Audit Success	Indicates An Audit Event
Computer:	SERVER1	The Server Name
Session_id:	52	The SPID
Server_Principal_Name:	SERVER1\John	The SQL Server Login
Database_Principal_Name:	dbo	The Database User
Server_Instance_Name:	SERVER1\SQLINSTANCEA	The SQL Server Instance
Database_Name:	HomeLending	The Database
Schema_Name:	dbo	The Database Object Schema
Object_Name:	Customer_Information	The Table Name
Statement:	Select * from customer_ information	The Statement That Was Executed.

Table 9-1: Critical auditing information captured the Windows Application Log.

The Windows Application Log can be located by navigating to the Windows Control Panel on the Start Menu and selecting Administrative Tools followed by Event Viewer. Within the event log, to the upper left, is an icon for the Windows Application Log.

It is useful to review the Windows Application Log to identify any events that have occurred on the decoy table, but it is a passive tool and depends upon the intentional review of the logs at a given point in time. Unless the DBA is constantly checking the logs, hours or days could pass before an event on the decoy table is identified. Instead, the DBA will need to create an alert that will notify the appropriate parties, through an e-mail or pager, when an event occurs.

Creating an Operator for Notification

The first step in creating a SQL Server alert is to create an Operator. An Operator is the person, or people, who will receive an alert when one is raised. We create an operator by executing the sp_add_operator system stored procedure in Management Studio. The following is an example of the syntax of this system stored procedure:

```
sp_add_operator [Operator Name],[Enabled],
                [Email Address],[Pager Address],
                [Weekday Pager Start],[Weekday Pager End],
                [Saturday Pager Start],[Saturday Pager End],
                [Sunday Pager Start],[Sunday Pager End],
                [Available Pager Days],[Netsend Address],
                [Category]
```

This system stored procedure's arguments are as follows:

- **Operator Name** – the textual reference to the Operator.

- **Enabled** – indicates whether the Operator can receive notifications.

- **Email Address** – the e-mail address to which notifications are sent for this Operator. This argument is only necessary when notifying through e-mail.

- **Pager Address** – all pager notifications are sent through the e-mail system. The value of this argument will need to be the e-mail account of the pager that will receive notifications. This argument is only necessary when notifying through a pager.

- **Weekday Pager Start/End** – the time of day during the weekday that notifications can be received. The value must be in the format of HHMMSS (Hour, Minute, Second). 0 indicates midnight. Despite this argument having the word "Pager" in it, it applies to e-mail

209

notifications as well. This argument is only necessary when the Operator is active on weekdays.

- **Saturday Pager Start/End** – the time of day on Saturday that notifications can be received. This argument is only necessary when the Operator is active on Saturdays.

- **Sunday Pager Start/End** – the time of day on Sunday that notifications can be received. This argument is only necessary when the Operator is active on Sundays.

- **Available Pager Days** – this indicates the days on which the Operator is available to receive notifications. This value ranges from 0 to 127. This value is determined by adding the assigned values of the days available. These assigned values are: Sunday (1), Monday (2), Tuesday (4), Wednesday (8), Thursday (16), Friday (32) and Saturday (64). For example: if an Operator is only available on Monday, Wednesday and Friday, this value would be 42 (2+8+32).

- **Netsend Address** – the network address to which a notification is to be sent. This argument is only necessary when notifying through net send.

- **Category** – the category of the Operator. This argument is optional.

Listing 9-6 shows how to create an operator for the DBA, called DBA1, in the msdb database. Of course, our intrepid DBA is always on call and so they are available everyday at all hours. Not that long ago, the DBA would have a pager strapped to them to receive very basic notifications. These days the availability of email, along with the multi-functional benefits of the cell phone, provide a means to receive a detailed email message quickly; therefore, the notification in our example will be sent via email.

```
USE msdb;
GO

EXEC msdb.dbo.sp_add_operator @name=N'DBA1',
        @enabled=1,
        @weekday_pager_start_time=0,
        @weekday_pager_end_time=235959,
        @saturday_pager_start_time=0,
        @saturday_pager_end_time=235959,
        @sunday_pager_start_time=0,
        @sunday_pager_end_time=235959,
```

```
        @pager_days=127,
        @email_address=N'DBA1@homelending.com';
GO
```

Listing 9-6: Creating an operator to receive notifications.

Creating an Alert for Notification

Once the operator has been created, we are ready to create our Alert. An Alert monitors the database for events. When an event occurs, a notification is sent to the Operators that are assigned to the Alert.

Alerts are dependent upon the SQL Server Agent, which must be running. If the SQL Server Agent is not running when an Alert is created, a message will be presented stating that it is not running and that the Alert will not function.

We can create alerts using the **sp_add_alert** system stored procedure, example syntax for which is as follows:

```
sp_add_alert [Alert Name],[Message ID],
             [Severity],[Enabled],
             [Delay Between Responses],[Notification Message],
             [Include Event Description In],[Database Name],
             [Event Description Keyword],[Job ID],
             [Job Name],[Raise SNMP Trap],
             [Performance Condition],[Category Name],
             [WMI Namespace], [WMI Query]
```

This system stored procedure's arguments are as follows:

- **Alert Name** – the textual reference to the Alert.

- **Message ID** – the value that identifies the message that is sent. In our case, our messages from the Server Audit are being captured in the Windows Application Log; therefore we can use the Error ID that is found in the sysmessages system table.

- **Severity** – the value that indicates the severity of the message sent. If the Message ID is used, this value must be 0.

- **Enabled** – indicates whether the Alert is active.

211

- **Delay Between Responses** – indicates the wait time for a notification to be sent after a previous notification. The value of 0 indicates that there is no delay.

- **Notification Message** – additional text that is sent with the event message. This is optional.

- **Include Event Description In** – identifies where the SQL Server event message should be provided. A value of 0 indicates that the SQL Server event message is not to be sent. A value of 1 indicates that it should be included in an e-mail. The other options that are available for this argument are noted to be removed in later versions of SQL Server and should be avoided.

- **Database Name** – the database where the event message will occur.

- **Event Description Keyword** – the pattern of characters that will occur in an event that will trigger a notification. This is necessary only when filtering events.

- **Job ID** – the id reference to the job that will be launched in response to the event. This is necessary only when launching a job in response to an event.

- **Job Name** – the textual reference to the job that will be launched in response to the event. This is necessary only when launching a job in response to an event.

- **Raise SNMP Trap** – indicates whether a Simple Network Management Protocol (SNMP) trap is raised in response to the event. This is optional and the default value is 0.

- **Performance Condition** – defines the performance conditions that will trigger a notification. This is necessary only when using performance events to raise the Alert.

- **Category Name** – the category of the Alert. This is optional.

- **WMI Namespace** – the Windows Management Instrumentation (WMI) namespace that is referenced by the WMI query. This is necessary only when using WMI events to raise the Alert.

- **WMI Query** – the query that identifies a WMI event that will trigger the alert. This is necessary only when using WMI events to raise the Alert.

Listing 9-7 creates a "Honeycomb Alert" in the msdb database.

```
USE msdb;
GO

EXEC msdb.dbo.sp_add_alert @name=N'Honeycomb Alert',
        @message_id=33205,
        @severity=0,
        @enabled=1,
        @delay_between_responses=0,
        @include_event_description_in=1,
        @database_name=N'HomeLending',
        @notification_message=N'Honeycomb Alert';
GO
```

Listing 9-7: Creating the Honeycomb Alert.

We are capturing our Server Audit events in the Windows Application Log; therefore we can use the message id of 33205 to identify that a Server Audit event has occurred.

Creating a Notification

Having created the Alert, Operators will need to be assigned to the Alert to receive notification messages. This can be accomplished by executing the sp_add_notification system stored procedure in Management Studio. The syntax of this system stored procedure is relatively straightforward:

```
sp_add_notification [Alert Name],[Operator Name],
                    [Notification Method]
```

This system stored procedure's arguments are:

- **Alert Name** – the textual reference to the Alert that will send a message.

- **Operator Name** – the textual reference to the Operator that will receive a message.

- **Notification Method** – identifies the method by which the message will be sent to the Operator. The values are: 1 (e-mail), 2 (pager), 4 (net send).

Listing 9-8 adds the Operator named DBA1 to the Honeycomb Alert Alert, and specifies that notification should be sent via e-mail.

```
USE msdb;
GO

EXEC msdb.dbo.sp_add_notification
    @alert_name=N'Honeycomb Alert',
    @operator_name=N'DBA1',
    @notification_method = 1;
GO
```

Listing 9-8: Creating the notification.

For this alert to be successful, the SQL Server Agent must be configured to send mail. This can be accomplished using the Database Mail Setup Wizard.

> **Avoid SQL Mail**
> **Please note that SQL Mail is a feature of SQL Server that is scheduled for retirement; therefore it is recommended to use Database Mail instead.**

The Database Mail Setup Wizard is accessible in Management Studio within the Management folder in Object Explorer; simply right-click on the "Database Mail" option and select "Configure Database Mail".

In order to make sure that everything is working as expected, it's worth sending a test e-mail; simply right-click the Database Mail option and select the "Send Test E-Mail ..." option.

Summary

By creating a honeycomb table, setting up auditing on that table, and enabling a means to be notified of an audit event, the Database Administrator can identify the precursors of an attack and respond quickly.

The audit feature of SQL Server 2008 is not limited to monitoring honeycomb tables. It also offers the ability to capture the occurrence of a wide array of events that occur on the database and instance giving the Database Administrator the proverbial "eyes in the back of the head" when identifying suspicious activities in the database that threaten the security of the sensitive data that is contained within it.

CHAPTER 10: LAYERING SOLUTIONS

When selecting the security methods that are to be applied to your database, it is important to understand the intended role of each method, within the overall security strategy. All methods have their particular strengths and vulnerabilities, and it is often possible to mitigate the latter.

However, any single security method, be it strategic schema design, encryption, obfuscation or role-based permissions, will ultimately fall short in the protection of sensitive data. In order to significantly reduce the risk of sensitive data being compromised, the DBA must implement a complex layering of security methods, strategically utilized and maintained within the database.

In the HomeLending database we used a few tables of our schema to illustrate these security methods; but what would this database look like if we were to fully implement the protection methods presented in this book throughout the entire database? In this final, short chapter, we'll take a moment to consider a fully implemented HomeLending database, based on all of the presented methods.

View from the Top Floor

At the highest level, we would want to consider the protection of our database files, including the database backups. In the SQL Server 2005 world, native options for protecting our physical database files, transaction logs and TempDB system database are non-existent. We would need to depend on features of the operating system, and on third party tools, for this level of protection. For example, Red Gate's SQL Backup Pro offers encryption of the backup files. In the world of SQL Server 2008, Enterprise Edition, the Transparent Data Encryption feature would be implemented, offering full protection for the physical files of the database, as well as its backup files.

Design for Protection

Figure 10-1 illustrates how the HomeLending database is organized into logical groupings. For example, the borrower names reside in the Borrower_Name table and the borrower's employer data resides in the Borrower_Employer table.

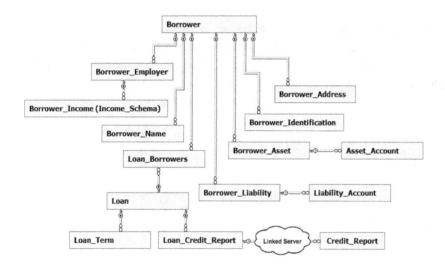

Figure 10-1: Schema design of the HomeLending database.

The Borrower_Identification, Borrower_Income, Asset_Account, Liability_Account and Credit_Report tables all contain sensitive data. Through the normalized design of the database, this sensitive data is separated from the non-sensitive data. The Credit_Report table takes advantage of a linked server to further the separation of sensitive data that is contained within that table.

Applied Permissions and Database Objects

The HomeLending database contains the database roles Sensitive_high, Sensitive_medium and Sensitive_low, which provides us the means to control access to database objects. Each database user that exists in the HomeLending database is assigned membership to one of these database roles.

To further elevate the level of overall security for the database, we deny access to the tables within the database to all database users. Accessing the data that is contained within the tables is granted through the creation of views. All INSERT, UPDATE and DELETE commands are funneled through stored procedures.

Cell-Level and One-Way Encryption

With the basic security features of SQL Server applied to the HomeLending database, the implementation of cell-level and one-way encryption can be observed.

The Borrower_Identification, Asset_Account and Liability_ Account tables utilize cell-level encryption to protect the identifying data and financial account numbers of the borrower. Thanks to the separation that was provided by the schema design, and the limited permissions that have been implemented to the views that access this data, the traffic to these columns does not have a noticeable impact on the performance of the database.

The cell-level encrypted columns take full advantage of the key hierarchy, including the use of the service master key, which not only provides cryptography without hard-coding passwords into user defined functions and stored procedures, but also prevents decryption on another SQL Server instance, with a different service master key.

Cell-level encryption does present a considerable performance hit when it is applied to data that is frequently searched. The encrypted Identification_ Value column, within the Borrower_Identification table, presents such a scenario. It is not uncommon to use a Social Security Number as a searchable field in which a borrower can be recalled.

The solution that we provide in the Borrower_Identification table is a second Identification_Value column, containing a salted one-way encrypted hash. Access to this column is provided to lower level database roles, by way of a stored procedure specifically designed to perform the hash comparison and return the search results.

Obfuscation

Underwriters would be a group of users that would fall into the `Sensitive_` `high` database role. These individuals review financial details and credit report details to determine if a borrower qualifies for the loan for which he or she has applied. Therefore, the `Sensitive_high` database role will be able to view the detailed credit report data contained in the `Credit_Report` linked table.

The Shipping Clerks represent a group of users that would fall into the `Sensitive_medium` database role. These individuals gather information about a loan that will be provided to potential investors. From this information the investors will decide to purchase the loan from the lender in the secondary market. There is no need for this group of users to view the details of the credit report. They are interested in aggregated versions of the data, such as the borrower's debt-to-income ratio, their credit score and the number of times that the borrower has been 30 days late with repayments. For the `Sensitive_` `medium` role, the obfuscation method of aggregation is a perfect solution. This would be offered through a view that is available to this database role.

Eyes in the Back of the Head

A honeycomb table, `Customer_Information`, and a database audit can be created to catch those who may snoop about for plain text sensitive data stored in the `HomeLending` database. Notification via database mail was set up to communicate the occurrence of any activity against this table to our DBA. For a bit of visual deterrence and intimidation, a silver hammer was provided to the DBA to whack anyone who may be found to have accessed the honeycomb table.

Good Habits

Performing regular backups of the database, as well as the encryption keys, will reduce the risk of data and key loss. Storing these backups separately will reduce the risk of theft of the data and the keys. Also, storing a duplicate copy of these backup files, at an offsite location, will reduce the risk of data loss due to a fire or natural disaster.

Devices and methods that protect data externally from the database, such as firewalls, secured network connections and user interface cryptography methods, are important for a broader security solution that involves data in transit.

Educate, Educate, Educate

Once the sensitive data has been secured within the database it is important to educate the users on how to recognize sensitive data and how it should and should not be communicated. The users will be the target for those who aim to circumvent your security efforts through social engineering and phishing attempts. These efforts to glean sensitive data can come from an external as well as an internal source.

Strong sensitive data handling policies, enforcement of these policies and continual education are the keys to protecting the data that has been entrusted to your business, to protecting the reputation of your business and, most importantly, protecting your customers.

Conclusion

In this book, we have explored the basic concepts of protecting sensitive data in SQL Server, and executed them against a sample HomeLending database.

Through this exploration, we have learned that all data is not created equally. There are many contributing factors that determine the sensitivity of a given piece of data. Regulations, industry standards and corporate policies are major resources in determining the sensitivity of data.

We have also learned that identity theft prevention, customer privacy, compliance with regulations, national security and even the survival of our businesses are some of the motivating factors that will result in the implementation of the measures discussed in this book.

The process of defining our sensitivity classes, evaluating each column in our database and assigning these classes to each of them provided us with the ability to apply the appropriate security measures and data handling policies consistently. The extended properties feature of SQL Server allowed us to document our data classification efforts. Through the use of catalog views and system stored procedures, the status of our classification definitions can be recalled on demand.

The completion of the data classification process led into the definition of database roles, and the assignment of database users as members of these roles provided the means by which we could efficiently control access to data in the various sensitivity classes.

With the data classification process complete, we began to explore the possibilities that the design of the schema can provide in our efforts to protect sensitive data. Normalization not only provided us with efficient storage and performance benefits, but also the separation of sensitive data from data of lower sensitivity classification.

Through the use of normalization, linked servers, views, permissions and database schema objects we discovered the tools that are available to improve the quality of our security and also to make the application of other security measures easier and more consistent.

Diving into the deep ocean of cryptography revealed to us the encryption features that are available in SQL Server. The menacing depth of cryptography was tamed through the discussion of some of the basic concepts as they apply to SQL Server.

Cell-level encryption, with its fine granularity, provided us with amazing control of sensitive data access and modification.

Transparent Data Encryption provided protection at a higher level by encrypting the physical files of the database. Through the higher level of security, the database files and our data are protected from being stolen and restored to another location.

One-way encryption granted us a means to encrypt our sensitive data without the need for decryption and key management. The myth of the invalidity of this option for protecting sensitive data has been broken and it is now an indispensible resource for our efforts.

We discovered that cryptography is not the only obfuscation method available to us in efforts to protect our sensitive data. Through the use of the string manipulation system functions, we could employ techniques such as character scrambling, repeating character masking, numeric variance, nulling and truncating. Additional methods of obfuscating sensitive data included encoding, aggregating and artificial data generation.

Thanks to the auditing feature of SQL Server 2008, we discovered honeycombing; the process of creating a decoy table to tempt potential attackers who are searching for sensitive data. By implementing a server audit and database audit specification on the honeycomb table the Database Administrator can identify that a potential attack may be underway before damage or disclosure occurs.

Finally, we have reviewed how all of these items can be applied to the HomeLending database to provide a layered model for the protection of sensitive data.

With this knowledge at hand, we can more effectively protect the sensitive data in our SQL Server database, protect the reputation of our businesses and protect the privacy of our clients.

"Privacy is not something that I'm merely entitled to, it's an absolute prerequisite." – Marlon Brando

222

Appendix A: Views and Functions Reference

Encryption Catalog Views Reference

All of the following catalog views, unless otherwise noted, are available in SQL Server 2005 as well as SQL Server 2008:

Sys.Asymmetric_Keys

The `sys.asymmetric_keys` catalog view presents the metadata for the asymmetric keys that exist in a database. This view can be executed against any user or system database within the SQL Server instance.

```
USE HomeLending;
GO

SELECT * FROM SYS.ASYMMETRIC_KEYS;
GO
```

Listing A-1: Syntax of `sys.asymmetric_keys`.

Sys.Certificates

The `sys.certificates` catalog view presents the metadata for the certificates that exist in a database. This view can be executed against any user or system database within the SQL Server instance.

```
USE HomeLending;
GO

SELECT * FROM SYS.CERTIFICATES;
GO
```

Listing A-2: Syntax of `sys.certificates`.

Sys.Credentials

The sys.credentials catalog view presents the metadata for the credentials that exist in an instance. Since credentials reside at the instance level, this must be executed against the master system database.

A credential provides a means for a SQL Server login to authenticate to a resource that is external from SQL Server, such as Windows Operating System or a cryptographic provider. A credential can have many SQL Server logins associated with it; but a SQL Server login can only have one credential associated with it.

```
USE master;
GO

SELECT * FROM SYS.CREDENTIALS;
GO
```

Listing A-3: Syntax of sys.credentials.

Sys.Crypt_Properties

The sys.crypt_properties catalog view presents the metadata for the properties regarding encryption for the objects in a database. This view can be executed against any user or system database within the SQL Server instance.

```
USE HomeLending;
GO

SELECT * FROM SYS.CRYPT_PROPERTIES;
GO
```

Listing A-4: Syntax of sys.crypt_properties.

Sys.Cryptographic_Providers

The sys.cryptographic_providers catalog view presents the metadata for the cryptographic providers that exist in an instance. Since credentials reside at the instance level, this must be executed against the master system database.

Cryptographic providers are specific to the Extensible Key Management (EKM) feature of SQL Server 2008 and are available only in that version. This feature is discussed in more detail later in this appendix.

```
USE master;
GO

SELECT * FROM SYS.CRYPTOGRAPHIC_PROVIDERS;
GO
```

Listing A-5: Syntax of `sys.cryptographic_providers`.

Sys.Key_Encryptions

The `sys.key_encryptions` catalog view presents the metadata for the keys that protect each symmetric key in the database. This view can be executed against any user or system database within the SQL Server instance.

```
USE HomeLending;
GO

SELECT * FROM SYS.KEY_ENCRYPTIONS;
GO
```

Listing A-6: Syntax of `sys.key_encryptions`.

Sys.OpenKeys

The `sys.openkeys` catalog view presents the encryption keys that have been opened in the current session and remain open. This view can be executed against any user or system database within the SQL Server instance.

```
USE HomeLending;
GO

SELECT * FROM SYS.OPENKEYS;
GO
```

Listing A-7: Syntax of `sys.openkeys`.

Sys.Symmetric_Keys

The `sys.symmetric_keys` catalog view presents the metadata for the symmetric keys that exist in a database. This view can be executed against any user or system database within the SQL Server instance.

```
USE HomeLending;
GO

SELECT * FROM SYS.SYMMETRIC_KEYS;
GO
```

Listing A-8: Syntax of `sys.symmetric_keys`.

Built-In Cryptographic Functions Reference

All of the following built-in cryptographic functions are available in SQL Server 2005 as well as SQL Server 2008:

AsymKey_ID

The built-in cryptographic functions that reference an asymmetric key, such as `EncryptByAsymKey` and `DecryptByAsymKey`, require the id of the key as a parameter. If the name of the asymmetric key is available, the id can be obtained through this function. The only argument for this function is the name of the asymmetric key that is being referenced.

```
USE HomeLending;
GO

SELECT AsymKey_ID('MyASymKey');
GO
```

Listing A-9: Syntax of **AsymKey_ID**.

Cert_ID

The built-in cryptographic functions that reference a certificate, such as EncryptByCert, DecryptByCert and CertProperty, require the id of the certificate as a parameter. If the name of the certificate is available, the id can be obtained through this function. The only argument for this function is the name of the certificate that is being referenced.

```
USE HomeLending;
GO

SELECT Cert_ID('MySelfSignedCert');
GO
```

Listing A-10: Syntax of Cert_ID.

CertProperty

A certification contains properties that are valuable for reference. Through this function the following properties can be returned:

- **Expiry_Date**: This is the date and time that the certificate is no longer available for use.

- **Start_Date**: This is the date and time that the certificate becomes available for use.

- **Issuer_Name**: The X.509 standard identifies the issuer as the entity that has verified the information within the certificate.

- **Cert_Serial_Number**: The X.509 standard defines this number as the value that uniquely identifies the certificate.

- **Subject**: The X.509 standard defines the subject as the person or entity that is identified with the certificate.

- **Sid**: The binary representation of the login security identifier for the certificate.

- **String_Sid**: The nvarchar representation of the login security identifier for the certificate.

```
USE HomeLending;
GO

SELECT CertProperty(Cert_ID('MySelfSignedCert'),'Expiry_
Date');
GO
```

Listing A-11: Syntax of `CertProperty`.

DecryptByAsymKey

This function is used to decrypt data that has been encrypted with an asymmetric key. The user performing decryption will require CONTROL permissions on the asymmetric key that is being referenced.

This function will return the decrypted value as a varbinary value, which will require the use of the CONVERT function to present the decrypted value as readable text.

```
USE HomeLending;
GO

SELECT
    Convert(nvarchar(max),
        DecryptByAsymKey(
            AsymKey_ID('MyASymKey'),
            Identification_Value,
            N'MyStr0ngP@ssword2009'
                    )
    )
FROM
    dbo.Borrower_Identification
WHERE
    Borrower_ID = 1;
GO
```

Listing A-12: Syntax of `DecryptByAsymKey`.

DecryptByCert

This function is used to decrypt data that has been encrypted with a certificate. The user performing decryption will require CONTROL permissions on the certificate that is being referenced.

This function will return the decrypted value as a varbinary value which will require the use of the CONVERT function to present the decrypted value as readable text.

```
USE HomeLending;
GO

SELECT
    Convert(nvarchar(max),
        DecryptByCert(
            Cert_ID('MySelfSignedCert'),
            Identification_Value,
            N'MyStr0ngP@ssword2009'
                )
    )
FROM
    dbo.Borrower_Identification
WHERE
    Borrower_ID = 1;
GO
```

Listing A-13: Syntax of DecryptByCert.

DecryptByKeyAutoAsymKey

Based upon the name of this function, you may assume that it would decrypt data using an asymmetric key; but it is actually used to decrypt data that was encrypted with a symmetric key. The asymmetric attribution in the function name reflects that the symmetric key itself is encrypted with an asymmetric key. This function is a hybrid of the OPEN SYMMETRIC KEY command, which is required for decrypting data, and the DecryptByKey function, which will be covered in more detail later in this appendix.

The user performing decryption will require CONTROL permissions on the asymmetric key that is being referenced to decrypt the symmetric key and VIEW DEFINITION permissions on the symmetric key that is used to perform the decryption of the data.

This function will return the decrypted value as a `varbinary` value, which will require the use of the `CONVERT` function to present the decrypted value as readable text.

```
USE HomeLending;
GO

SELECT
    Convert(nvarchar(max),
        DecryptByKeyAutoAsymKey(
            AsymKey_ID('MyASymKey'),
                        NULL,
            1,
            N'MySymKeyAuthenticator'
                )
    )
FROM
    dbo.Borrower_Identification
WHERE
    Borrower_ID = 1;
GO
```

Listing A-14: Syntax of `DecryptByKeyAutoAsymKey`.

DecryptByKeyAutoCert

Based upon the name of this function you may assume that it would decrypt data using a certificate key; but it is actually used to decrypt data that was encrypted with a symmetric key. The certificate attribution in the function name reflects that the symmetric key itself is encrypted with a certificate. This function is a hybrid of the `OPEN SYMMETRIC KEY` command, which is required for decrypting data, and the `DecryptByKey` function, which will be covered in more detail later in this appendix.

The user performing decryption will require `CONTROL` permissions on the certificate that is being referenced to decrypt the symmetric key and `VIEW DEFINITION` permissions on the symmetric key that is used to perform the decryption of the data.

```
USE HomeLending;
GO

SELECT
    Convert(nvarchar(max),
        DecryptByKeyAutoCert(
            Cert_ID('MySelfSignedCert'),
                        NULL,
            1,
            N'MySymKeyAuthenticator'
                )
    )
FROM
    dbo.Borrower_Identification
WHERE
    Borrower_ID = 1;
GO
```

Listing A-15: Syntax of `DecryptByKeyAutoCert`.

DecryptByKey

This function is used to decrypt data that has been encrypted with a symmetric key. The execution of this function is dependent upon the symmetric key being opened prior to its call.

The user performing decryption will require VIEW DEFINITION permissions on the symmetric key that is being referenced. If the symmetric key itself is encrypted by a certificate or asymmetric key, CONTROL permissions on the certificate or asymmetric key is required.

This function will return the decrypted value as a varbinary value, which will require the use of the CONVERT function to present the decrypted value as readable text.

NOTE:

To use symmetric keys in the encryption and decryption process they must first be opened. Once the key is opened, using the OPEN SYMMETRIC KEY command, it remains open until it is explicitly closed, using the CLOSE SYMMETRIC KEY command, or the session is terminated.

```
USE HomeLending;
GO

OPEN SYMMETRIC KEY MySymKey
    DECRYPT BY PASSWORD = N'MyStr0ngP@ssword2009';
GO

SELECT
    Convert(nvarchar(max),
        DecryptByKey(Identification_Value)
    )
FROM
    dbo.Borrower_Identification
WHERE
    Borrower_ID = 1;
GO

CLOSE SYMMETRIC KEY MySymKey;
GO
```

Listing A-16: Syntax of `DecryptByKey`.

DecryptByPassphrase

This function is used to decrypt data that has been encrypted with a key that is generated from a passphrase. The user performing decryption will require the knowledge of the passphrase that was used during the encryption process.

This function will return the decrypted value as a `varbinary` value, which will require the use of the CONVERT function to present the decrypted value as readable text.

```
USE HomeLending;
GO

SELECT
    Convert(nvarchar(max),
        DecryptByPassphrase(
            'The Crow Flies At Midnight.',
            Identification_Value
            )
    )
FROM
    dbo.Borrower_Identification
```

```
WHERE
    Borrower_ID = 1;
GO
```

Listing A-17: Syntax of `DecryptByPassphrase`.

EncryptByAsymKey

This function is used to encrypt data with an asymmetric key. No specific permissions need to be granted to a user in order to use this function.

```
USE HomeLending;
GO

UPDATE dbo.Borrower_Identification
    SET Identification_Value =
                EncryptByAsymKey(
                AsymKey_ID('MyASymKey'),
                Identification_Value
                          )
WHERE
    Borrower_ID = 1;
GO
```

Listing A-18: Syntax of `EncryptByAsymKey`.

EncryptByCert

This function is used to encrypt data with a certificate. No specific permissions need to be granted to a user in order to use this function.

```
USE HomeLending;
GO

UPDATE dbo.Borrower_Identification
    SET Identification_Value =
                EncryptByCert(
                Cert_ID('MySelfSignedCert'),
                Identification_Value
                          )
WHERE
    Borrower_ID = 1;
GO
```

Listing A-19: Syntax of `EncryptByCert`.

EncryptByKey

This function is used to encrypt data with a symmetric key. The execution of this function is dependent upon the symmetric key being opened prior to its call.

```
USE HomeLending;
GO

OPEN SYMMETRIC KEY MySymKey
    DECRYPT BY PASSWORD = N'MyStr0ngP@ssword2009';
GO

UPDATE dbo.Borrower_Identification
    SET Identification_Value =
                EncryptByKey(
                    Key_GUID('MySymKey'),
                    Identification_Value
                    )
WHERE
    Borrower_ID = 1;
GO

CLOSE SYMMETRIC KEY MySymKey;
GO
```

Listing A-20: Syntax of `EncryptByKey`.

EncryptByPassphrase

This function is used to encrypt data with a key that is generated from a passphrase.

```
USE HomeLending;
GO

UPDATE dbo.Borrower_Identification
    SET Identification_Value =
                EncryptByPassphrase (
                    'The Crow Flies At Midnight.',
                    Identification_Value
                    )
WHERE
    Borrower_ID = 1;
GO
```

Listing A-21: Syntax of `EncryptByPassphrase`.

Key_ID

The catalog views that reference a symmetric key, such as `sys.symmetric_keys` and `sys.key_encryptions`, can have their results filtered based off the id of the symmetric key. If the name of the symmetric key is available, the id can be obtained through this function. The only argument for this function is the name of the symmetric key that is being referenced.

```
USE HomeLending;
GO

SELECT Key_ID('MySymKey');
GO
```

Listing A-22: Syntax of Key_ID.

Key_GUID

The built-in cryptographic functions that reference a symmetric key, such as `DecryptByKey`, require the globally unique identifier of the symmetric key as a parameter. If the name of the symmetric key is available, the globally unique identifier can be obtained through this function. The only argument for this function is the name of the symmetric key that is being referenced.

```
USE HomeLending;
GO

SELECT Key_GUID('MySymKey');
GO
```

Listing A-23: Syntax of Key_GUID.

SignByAsymKey

This function digitally signs the plain text data that is passed through its arguments with an asymmetric key. This function is often used in conjunction with the `EncryptByAsymKey` function.

Successful digital signing requires the user to have CONTROL permissions on the asymmetric key that is being used to generate the digital signature.

235

```
USE HomeLending;
GO

UPDATE dbo.Borrower_Identification
    SET Identification_Value =
                EncryptByAsymKey(
                    AsymKey_ID('MyASymKey'),
                Identification_Value
                            ),
                Value_DigSig =
                    SignByAsymKey (
                                AsymKey_ID('MyASymKey'),
                Identification_Value,
                                N'MyStr0ngP@ssw0rd2009'
                            )
WHERE
    Borrower_ID = 1;
GO
```

Listing A-24: Syntax of **SignByAsymKey**.

SignByCert

This function digitally signs the plain text data that is passed through its arguments with a certificate. This function is often used in conjunction with the EncryptByCert function.

Successful digital signing requires the user to have CONTROL permissions on the certificate that is being used to generate the digital signature.

```
USE HomeLending;
GO

UPDATE dbo.Borrower_Identification
    SET Identification_Value =
                EncryptByCert(
                Cert_ID('MySelfSignedCert'),
                Identification_Value
                            ),
```

```
               Value_DigSig =
                 SignByCert (
                             Cert_ID('MySelfSignedCert'),
                 Identification_Value,
                             N'MyStr0ngP@ssw0rd2009'
                             )
WHERE
   Borrower_ID = 1;
GO
```

Listing A-25: Syntax of `SignByCert`.

VerifySignedByAsymKey

This function determines if the encrypted data has changed since it was
digitally signed. The returned value is either a 1, which indicates that the data
has not changed, or 0 which indicates that the data has changed. This function
is often used in conjunction with the `DecryptByAsymKey` function.

Successful digital signature verification requires the user to have `VIEW`
`DEFINITION` permissions on the asymmetric key that was used to generate the
digital signature.

```
USE HomeLending;
GO

SELECT
      VerifySignedByAsymKey(
      AsymKey_ID('MyASymKey'),
         Convert(nvarchar(max),
      DecryptByAsymKey(
         AsymKey_ID('MyASymKey'),
         Identification_Value,
         N'MyStr0ngP@ssword2009'
            )
      ),
         N'MyStr0ngP@ssword2009'
      )
FROM
   dbo.Borrower_Identification
WHERE
   Borrower_ID = 1;
GO
```

Listing A-26: Syntax of `VerifySignedByAsymKey`.

VerifySignedByCert

This function determines if the encrypted data has changed since it was digitally signed. The returned value is either a 1, which indicates that the data has not changed, or 0 which indicates that the data has changed. This function is often used in conjunction with the DecryptByCert function.

Successful digital signature verification requires the user to have VIEW DEFINITION permissions on the certificate that was used to generate the digital signature.

```
USE HomeLending;
GO

SELECT
        VerifySignedByCert(
      Cert_ID('MySelfSignedCert'),
            Convert(nvarchar(max),
      DecryptByCert(
         Cert_ID('MySelfSignedCert'),
         Identification_Value,
         N'MyStr0ngP@ssword2009'
                )
         ),
            N'MyStr0ngP@ssword2009'
         )
FROM
   dbo.Borrower_Identification
WHERE
   Borrower_ID = 1;
GO
```

Listing A-27: Syntax of `VerifySignedByCert`.

String Manipulation Function Reference

All of the following system functions provide support for the ability to manipulate strings of characters that is available in SQL Server 2005 as well as SQL Server 2008:

238

ASCII and CHAR

The ASCII and CHAR system functions provide the conversion functionality between character values and ASCII code values. These system functions are valuable when iterating through characters, mathematically determining characters and randomly deriving characters.

The American Standard Code for Information Interchange (ASCII) is a coding scheme that is used by computers. The ASCII codes range from 0 to 255. The ASCII codes for the standard, upper case, English alphabet ranges from 65 (A) to 90 (Z). The ASCII codes for the standard, lower case, English alphabet ranges from 97 (a) to 122 (z).

The ASCII system function returns the ASCII code value of a given character. The argument to this function is the character to which the ASCII code is requested. For example, passing the value of "A" will return the value of 65.

The CHAR system function returns the character of a given ASCII value. The argument to this function is the ASCII code to which the character value is requested. For example, passing the value of 65 will return the value of "A".

```
--Returns "65"
SELECT ASCII('A');
GO

--Returns "A"
SELECT CHAR(65);
GO
```

Listing A-28: The ASCII and CHAR functions.

LEFT, RIGHT and SUBSTRING

The LEFT, RIGHT and SUBSTRING system functions provide the functionality of obtaining a portion of a value. These system functions are valuable for concatenating a portion of a value to another string during masking processes.

The LEFT system function returns a portion of the value passed, based upon a defined number of characters from its beginning, or left most character. The value returned is either a varchar (for non-unicode values) or nvarchar (for unicode values) data type.

The RIGHT system function returns a portion of the value passed, based upon a defined number of characters from its ending, or right most character. The value returned is either a varchar (for non-unicode values) or nvarchar (for unicode values) data type.

The arguments for the LEFT and RIGHT system functions are:

- **Expression**: This is the value in which a portion will be returned. The data type can be any type that can be implicitly converted to varchar or nvarchar data types.

- **Characters_To_Return**: This is the number of characters that are to be returned.

The SUBSTRING system function returns a portion of the value passed, based upon a defined number of characters from a defined beginning position within the value. The value returned can be varchar, nvarchar, or varbinary, depending upon the data type of the value passed into the system function.

The arguments for the SUBSTRING system function are:

- **Expression**: This is the value in which a portion will be returned. The data type can be any type that can be implicitly converted to varchar or nvarchar data types.

- **Start_Position**: This is a number that represents the position within the expression that will define the starting point of the value to be returned.

- **Characters_To_Return**: This is the number of characters that are to be returned.

```
--Returns "This"
SELECT LEFT('This is a string',4);
GO
--Returns "ring"
SELECT RIGHT('This is a string',4);
GO

--Returns "a st"
SELECT SUBSTRING('This is a string',9,4);
GO
```

Listing A-29: **LEFT**, **RIGHT**, and **SUBSTRING** functions.

REPLACE

The REPLACE system function provides the functionality of replacing all occurrences of a given value with another value. This system function is valuable for masking processes. If the value that is passed into this system function is an nvarchar data type, the value returned will be nvarchar; otherwise this will return a varchar data type.

The arguments for the REPLACE system function are:

- **Expression**: This is the value that is to be evaluated in this system function. The data type can be any type that can be implicitly converted to varchar or nvarchar data types.

- Search_Pattern: This is the value that is being sought within the expression to be replaced.

- Replace_Pattern: This is the value that will replace the search pattern when found.

```
--Returns "Thwas was a string"
SELECT REPLACE('This is a string','is','was');
GO
```

Listing A-30: Using the REPLACE function.

REPLICATE and SPACE

The REPLICATE and SPACE system functions provide the functionality of repeating a value for a number of iterations. These system functions are valuable during masking processes.

The REPLICATE system function returns a given value for a given number of iterations. The data type that is returned is the same as the data type passed into the expression argument. The maximum iterations that will be returned are 8,000.

The arguments for the REPLICATE system function are:

- **Expression**: This is the value that is to be evaluated in this system function.

- **Iteration_Count**: This is the number of iterations to which the expression is to be repeated.

241

The SPACE system function returns a space (" ") for a given number of iterations. The data type that is returned is char. The maximum iterations that will be returned are 8,000. If the resulting value is to be concatenated to unicode values, the REPLICATE system function should be used instead of the SPACE system function.

The arguments for the SPACE system function are:

- **Iteration_Count**: This is the number of iterations to which a space is to be repeated.

```
--Returns "XXXXXXXXXX"
SELECT REPLICATE('X',10);
GO

--Returns "          "
SELECT SPACE(10);
GO
```

Listing A-31: Using REPLICATE and SPACE .

REVERSE

The REVERSE system function provides the functionality of reversing the order of characters that are contained in a given value. This system function is valuable for masking processes. If the value that is passed into this system function is of the nvarchar data type, the value returned will be nvarchar; otherwise this will return a varchar data type.

The arguments for the REVERSE system function are:

- **Expression**: This is the value that is to be evaluated in this system function. The data type can be any type that can be implicitly converted to varchar or nvarchar data types.

```
--Returns "gnirts a si sihT"
SELECT REVERSE('This is a string');
GO
```

Listing A-32: REVERSE a string.

STUFF

The STUFF system function provides the functionality inserting a given value into another given value, replacing a given number of characters. This system function is valuable for masking processes. The data type that is returned is the same as the data type passed into the expression argument.

The arguments for the STUFF system function are:

- **Expression**: This is the value that is to be evaluated in this system function.

- **Start_Position**: This is a number that represents the position within the expression that the inserting value will be inserted.

- **Delete_Characters**: This is a number that represents the characters that will be removed from the expression when the inserting value is placed.

- **Inserting_Value**: This is the value that will be inserted into the expression.

```
--Returns "ThBubba is a string"
SELECT STUFF('This is a string',3,2,'Bubba');
GO
```

Listing A-33: STUFF a string.

RAND

The RAND system function, when called, returns a random value of the float data type.

The only argument for the RAND system function is **Seed**, which is the value that defines the starting point in which the random number is derived. If the system function is called repeatedly with the same seed value it will always return the same value. If this argument is not included, the database engine will produce a random seed value.

```
-- With a seed value defined
-- Will always return 0.715436657367485
SELECT RAND(100);
```

Listing A-34: Using the RAND function.

243

Appendix B: The HomeLending

Database

Throughout this book, a sample database, called HomeLending, is used to illustrate the security, schema design, encryption and obfuscation methods that are available in SQL Server. All of the coding examples that are provided in this book were written using **SQL Server 2008 SP1, Developer Edition**.

The script that is used to create the HomeLending database as well as all of the examples provided in this book can be found at the following URL:

http://www.simple-talk.com/RedGateBooks/JohnMagnabosco/HLSchema.zip

Within the downloaded compressed folder are the following files:

Database Creation Scripts

- **CreateHomeLendingDB.sql**
  This file will create the physical files (.mdf/.ldf) for the HomeLending database.

- **CreateHomeLendingTables.sql**
  This file will create the tables for the HomeLending database.

- **CreateHomeLendingRelationships.sql**
  This file will create the relationships for the tables of the HomeLending database.

Database Roles, Users and Schema Scripts

- **CreateRolesUsers_Chapter2.sql**
  This file will create the database roles, users and role memberships for the HomeLending database.

- **ExtendedProperties_Chapter2.sql**
  This file will create the extended properties for the HomeLending database table columns.

- **ArchitectureStrategies_Chapter3.sql**
  This file will create database schema objects, views and linked servers.

Encryption Scripts

- **CreateKeysCerts_Chapter4.sql**
  This file will create encryption keys and certificates.

- **CreateCryptographicProvider_Chapter4.sql**
  (SS2008 Only)
  This file will create a cryptographic provider for the Extensible Key Management feature.

- **BackupKeysCerts_Chapter4.sql**
  This file will back up the encryption keys and certificates.

- **CellLevelEncryption_Chapter5.sql**
  This file will implement cell-level encryption on a single column in the HomeLending database.

- **TransparentDataEncryption_Chapter6.sql** *(SS2008 Only)*
  This file will implement transparent data encryption for the HomeLending database.

- **TDERestoreReversal_Chapter6.sql**
  This file will restore and reverse the implementation of TDE.

- **OneWayEncryption_Chapter7.sql**
  This file will implement one-way encryption.

Obfuscation and Honeycombing Scripts

- Obfuscation_Chapter8.sql
  This file will create various obfuscation methods.

- **Honeycombing_Chapter9.sql** *(SS2008 Only)*
  This file will create a honeycomb table as well as a database audit.

Please note that it is highly discouraged to implement the provided sample code, either entirely or in part, on an instance of SQL Server that is actively utilized for production activity. All sample code is provided for illustrative purposes only and are provided "as is" without any warranties or guarantees of any kind, either expressed or implied. In no event shall the author or publisher be liable for any direct, indirect, incidental, special, exemplary, or consequential damages arising in any way out of the use of the provided sample code.

Creating the HomeLending Database

To create the HomeLending database, perform the following instructions:

- **Download** the compressed folder **HLSchema.zip** from the previously provided URL.

- **Open SQL Server Management Studio** (SSMS) and connect to the desired SQL Server instance.

- Open the file named CreateHomeLendingDB.sql in SSMS.

- **Modify** the FILENAME argument in the CREATE DATABASE command to the desired location of the database's **.mdf** and **.ldf** files.

- **Execute** the script.

If SSMS is not available in the start menu, you can typically find the location of this program at:

SQL Server 2008 SSMS:
C:\Program Files\Microsoft SQL Server\100\Tools\Binn\VSShell\Common7\IDE\Ssms.exe

SQL Server 2005 SSMS:
C:\Program Files\Microsoft SQL Server\90\Tools\Binn\VSShell\Common7\IDE\SqlWb.exe

Creating the HomeLending Database Tables

Once the script for the `HomeLending` database has been successfully completed, the tables can be created through the following instructions:

- **Open the file** named `CreateHomeLendingTables.sql` in SSMS.

- **Execute** the script.

- **Open the file** named `CreateHomeLendingRelationships.sql` in SSMS to create the foreign keys for the newly created tables.

- **Execute** the script.

At this point the `HomeLending` database has been created; but is empty. It is recommended to use a tool, such as Red Gate's SQL Data Generator, to produce the data for this sample. Many of these tools make their best guess as to the format of the data that is being populated. You may want to review these definitions and modify them as needed to populate your database with data that has the appearance of real data.

You can download a trial of Red Gate's SQL Data Generator at:
http://www.red-gate.com/products/SQL_Data_Generator/index.htm

Executing Subsequent Scripts

As you progress through this book there will be sample code provided that can be used on the `HomeLending` database. Simply perform the following to execute these scripts:

- **Open** the desired script file in SSMS.

- **Execute** the desired portion of the script.

There are some scripts that reference a physical location through a drive and folder specification. Please modify these according to your environment prior to execution.

INDEX

Symbols

128-bit RC4 101
.bak 138
@@IDENTITY 132
.ldf 138
.mdf 138

A

abstraction 67
Administrative Tools 208
Advanced Encryption Standard 100
AES
  AES 128 100
  AES 192 100
  AES 256 100
aggregated data 28, 199
Aggregating 187
Alert 211
algorithm 37, 89
ALL 52
ALTER 49
ALTER ANY USER 48
ALTER TABLE 123, 171
ANSI-92 51
Application Role 44
ArchitectureStrategies_Chapter3.sql 246
argument 77
Artificial Data Generation 187
ASCII (American Standard Code for
  Information Interchange)
  239
AsymKey_ID 103, 226
asymmetric key 46, 91
Attack Dictionary 163
auditing 203
Australian Privacy Act, 1988 27
AUTHORIZATION 77

B

Backup
  BACKUP CERTIFICATE 98, 142,
    145

back up files 75
BackupKeysCerts_Chapter4.sql 246
BACKUP MASTER KEY 98, 142
backup media 142
BACKUP SERVICE MASTER KEY
  98, 142
Behavioral biometrics 27
biometric data 26
Biometric Institute Privacy Code 27
Birthday Paradox 166
block cipher 100
boot record 142
built-in cryptographic functions 226

C

California Information Practices Act 29
Canada, Personal Information Protection
  and Electronic Information Act 19
catalog view 54, 223
cell-level encryption xvii
CellLevelEncryption_Chapter5.sql 246
Cert_I 227
Cert_ID 103
certificate 46, 91
CertProperty 103, 228
CHAR 239
Character
  Character_Mask 191
  Character_Scramble 189
  character scrambling 185, 187
checkpoint 143
Chief Information Officer 64
Chief Security Officer 64
Children's Online Privacy Protection Act,
  1988 29
cipher text 89
CLOSE SYMMETRIC KEY 131
CLR 104
COALESCE 128
Company Tax Reference (UK) 25
complex joins 79
confidentiality 69
Configure Database Mail 214
CONTROL 53

249

SQL Tools
from **Red Gate Software**

ingeniously simple tools

SQL Backup   from **$295**

Compress, encrypt and monitor SQL Server backups

- ↗ Compress database backups by **up to 95%** for faster backups and restores
- ↗ Protect your data with up to 256-bit AES encryption (SQL Backup Pro only)
- ↗ Monitor your data with an interactive timeline, so you can check and edit the status of past, present and future backup activities
- ↗ Optimize backup performance with multiple threads in SQL Backup's engine

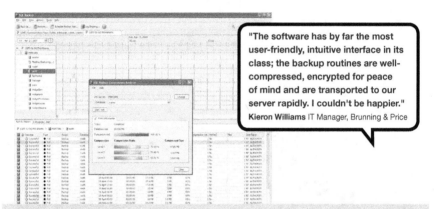

"The software has by far the most user-friendly, intuitive interface in its class; the backup routines are well-compressed, encrypted for peace of mind and are transported to our server rapidly. I couldn't be happier."
Kieron Williams IT Manager, Brunning & Price

SQL Response   from **$495**

Monitors SQL Servers, with alerts and diagnostic data

- ↗ Investigate long-running queries, SQL deadlocks, blocked processes and more to resolve problems sooner
- ↗ Intelligent email alerts notify you as problems arise, without overloading you with information
- ↗ Concise, relevant data provided for each alert raised
- ↗ Low-impact monitoring and no installation of components on your SQL Servers

"SQL Response enables you to monitor, get alerted and respond to SQL problems before they start, in an easy-to-navigate, user-friendly and visually precise way, with drill-down detail where you need it most."
H John B Manderson President and Principle Consultant, Wireless Ventures Ltd

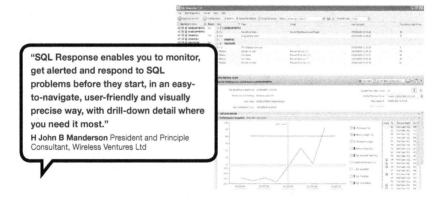

SQL Compare

from **$395**

Compare and synchronize SQL Server database schemas

↗ Automate database comparisons, and synchronize your databases
↗ Simple, easy to use, 100% accurate
↗ Save hours of tedious work, and eliminate manual scripting errors
↗ Work with live databases, snapshots, script files or backups

> "SQL Compare and SQL Data Compare
> are the best purchases we've made in the
> .NET/SQL environment. They've saved us
> hours of development time and the fast,
> easy-to-use database comparison gives
> us maximum confidence that our migration
> scripts are correct. We rely on these
> products for every deployment."
>
> **Paul Tebbutt** Technical Lead, Universal Music Group

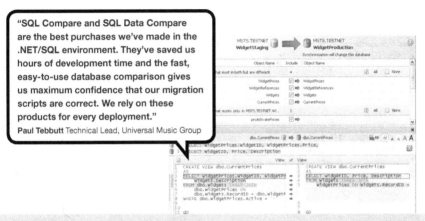

SQL Data Compare

from **$395**

Compare and synchronize SQL Server database schemas

↗ Compare your database contents
↗ Automatically synchronize your data
↗ Simplify data migrations
↗ Row-level restore
↗ Compare to backups

SQL Prompt

from $195

Intelligent code completion and layout for SQL Server

- ↗ Write SQL fast and accurately with code completion
- ↗ Understand code more easily with script layout
- ↗ Continue to use your current editor – SQL Prompt works within SSMS, Query Analyzer, and Visual Studio
- ↗ Keyword formatting, join completion, code snippets, and many more powerful features

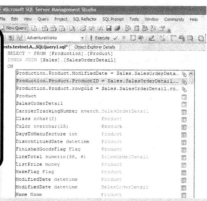

"It's amazing how such a simple concept quickly becomes a way of life. With SQL Prompt there's no longer any need to hunt out the design documentation, or to memorize every field length in the entire database. It's about freeing the mind from being a database repository - and instead concentrate on problem solving and solution providing!" **Dr Michael Dye** Dyetech

SQL Data Generator

$295

Test data generator for SQL Server databases

- ↗ Data generation in one click
- ↗ Realistic data based on column and table name
- ↗ Data can be customized if desired
- ↗ Eliminates hours of tedious work

"Red Gate's SQL Data Generator has overnight become the principal tool we use for loading test data to run our performance and load tests"
Grant Fritchey Principal DBA, FM Global

Preview of data to be generated (first 100 lines)

TitleOfCourtesy Title	BirthDate datetime	HireDate datetime	Address Address Line (Stre	City US City	Region Region	PostalCode ZIP Code	Country Country	HomeP Phone
Dr	23/08/1963 04:0...	25/04/1992 20:0...	37 Fabien St.	Richmond	IA-CT	58907	Gibraltar	12353:
Miss	10/01/1960 23:2...	16/02/1976 11:2...	850 White Nobel...	NULL	NV-EW	39330	Tajikistan	69862:
Mr	27/07/1970 13:5...	03/12/1953 15:3...	45 Green Milton...	New York	TN-OH	60387	Liberia	529-89
Mr	27/01/2002 04:3...	24/07/1958 00:5...	43 Milton Boulev	Sacramento	NM-JR	13294	Côte d'Ivoire	984-11
Mr	31/05/1994 04:1...	12/01/1964 04:4...	592 Rocky Cowl...	Santa Ana	MI-UU	NULL	Jersey	417-47
Mrs	17/11/1975 10:1...	27/10/1968 18:5...	69 Clarendon Pa...	San Jose	IL-TC	41768	New Caledonia	11305(
Dr.	16/05/1974 06:1...	25/11/1998 14:5...	207 Fabien Blvd.	Houston	AL-GE	04937	Belgium	896878
Dr	27/12/1999 19:4...	03/05/1972 13:1...	53 Rocky Oak R...	Baton Rouge	MA-RT	65364	Swaziland	076-87
Dr	14/10/1971 03:1...	28/06/1978 10:0...	260 East Rocky...	Charlotte	AL-AR	97727	Benin	54684!
Mr	09/11/1981 13:2...	26/12/2001 15:0...	476 North Fabie...	Akron	MA-IU	94269	Palau	875611
Dr	28/06/1987 01:3...	30/10/1972 00:0...	48 South Hague...	Norfolk	VT-UV	66385	American Samoa	89085(
Mr	20/10/1962 04:4...	07/09/2005 17:1...	939 Fabien Park...	Grand Rapids	HI-YT	86033	Swaziland	58415(
Mr	25/01/2001 08:0...	18/08/1983 12:0...	348 North Green...	Wichita	FL-IV	32302	Zambia	124-42
Mr	05/01/1955 10:0...	12/08/1983 22:5...	32 Cowley Boule...	Spokane	WV-DI	45980	Chile	457-22

SQL Toolbelt™ $1,795

The twelve essential SQL Server tools for database professionals

You can buy our acclaimed SQL Server tools individually or bundled.
Our most popular deal is the SQL Toolbelt: all twelve SQL Server tools in a single installer, with **a combined value of $5,240 but an actual price of $1,795**, a saving of more than 65%.

*Fully compatible with SQL Server 2000, 2005 and **2008!***

SQL Doc

Intelligent code completion and layout for SQL Server

↗ Produce simple, legible and fast HTML reports for multiple databases
↗ Documentation is stored as part of the database
↗ Output completed documentation to a range of different formats.

$295

SQL Dependency Tracker

The graphical tool for tracking database and cross-server dependencies

↗ Visually track database object dependencies
↗ Discover all cross-database and cross-server object relationships
↗ Analyze potential impact of database schema changes
↗ Rapidly document database dependencies for reports, version control, and database change planning

$195

SQL Packager

Compress and package your databases for easy installations and upgrades

↗ Script your entire database accurately and quickly
↗ Move your database from A to B
↗ Compress your database as an exe file, or launch as a Visual Studio project
↗ Simplify database deployments and installations

from $295

SQL Multi Script

Single-click script execution on multiple SQL Servers

↗ Cut out repetitive administration by deploying multiple scripts on multiple servers with just one click
↗ Return easy-to-read, aggregated results from your queries to export either as a csv or .txt file
↗ Edit queries fast with an intuitive interface, including colored syntax highlighting, Find and Replace, and split-screen editing

$195

SQL Comparison SDK

Automate database comparisons and synchronizations

↗ Full API access to Red Gate comparison tools
↗ Incorporate comparison and synchronization functionality into your applications
↗ Schedule any of the tasks you require from the SQL Comparison Bundle

$595

SQL Refactor

Refactor and format your SQL code

Twelve tools to help update and maintain databases quickly and reliably, including:

↗ Rename object and update all references
↗ Expand column wildcards, qualify object names, and uppercase keywords
↗ Summarize script
↗ Encapsulate code as stored procedure

$295

How to Become an Exceptional DBA
Brad McGehee

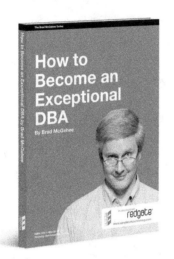

A career guide that will show you, step-by-step, exactly what you can do to differentiate yourself from the crowd so that you can be an Exceptional DBA. While Brad focuses on how to become an Exceptional SQL Server DBA, the advice in this book applies to any DBA, no matter what database software they use. If you are considering becoming a DBA, or are a DBA and want to be more than an average DBA, this is the book to get you started.

ISBN: 978-1-906434-05-2
Published: July 2008

SQL Server Execution Plans
Grant Fritchey

Execution plans show you what's going on behind the scenes in SQL Server and provide you with a wealth of information on how your queries are being executed. Grant provides a clear route through the subject, from the basics of capturing plans, through their interpretation, and then right on to how to use them to understand how you might optimize your SQL queries, improve your indexing strategy, and so on. All this rich information makes the execution plan a fairly important tool in the tool belt of pretty much anyone who writes TSQL to access data in a SQL Server database.

ISBN: 978-1-906434-02-1
Published: June 2008

Mastering SQL Server Profiler
Brad McGehee

For such a potentially powerful tool, Profiler is surprisingly underused; unless you have a lot of experience as a DBA, it is often hard to analyze the data you capture. As such, many DBAs tend to ignore it and this is distressing, because Profiler has so much potential to make a DBA's life more productive. SQL Server Profiler records data about various SQL Server events, and this data can be used to troubleshoot a wide range of SQL Server issues, such as poorly-performing queries, locking and blocking, excessive table/index scanning, and a lot more.

ISBN: 978-1-906434-15-1
Published: January 2009

Two Minute SQL Server Stumpers

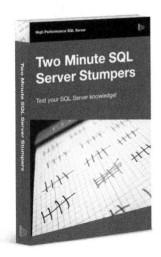

Challenge yourself in a variety of ways about the different aspects of SQL Server. Some of the questions are arcane, some very common, but you'll learn something and the wide range of questions will help you get your mind agile and ready for some quick thinking. This version is a compilation of SQL Server 2005 and SQL Server 2008 questions, to bring you up to date on the latest version of SQL Server. So read on, in order, randomly, just start going through them, but do yourself a favor and think about each before turning the page. Challenge yourself and see how well you do.

ISBN: 978-1-906434-21-2
Published: August 2009